BUSINESS SCHOOL

CONFIDENTIAL

ALSO BY ROBERT H. MILLER

Law School Confidential

BUSINESS SCHOOL CONFIDENTIAL

A Complete Guide to the
Business School Experience:
By Students, for Students

Robert H. Miller
and Katherine F. Koegler

Foreword by Charles F. Knight

THOMAS DUNNE BOOKS
ST. MARTIN'S GRIFFIN

THOMAS DUNNE BOOKS.
An imprint of St. Martin's Press.

www.stmartins.com

Photos of mentors and authors courtesy of Amy Belt, David Bussa,
Matt Fates, Kanna Kunchala, David Liebowicz, Carolyn K. Miller,
Brent S. Riggi, Anne Walker Ruiz, Andy Stewart, Toby D. Stickler, and
Alden M. Whittaker.

LIBRARY OF CONGRESS CATALOGING-IN-PUBLICATION DATA

Miller, Robert H. (Robert Harrax)
    Business school confidential : a complete guide to the business
school experience : by students, for students / Robert H. Miller
and Katherine F. Koegler; foreword by Charles F. Knight.
        p. cm.
    ISBN 0-312-30086-7
    1. Business education—United States.   2. Business schools—
United States.   3. Business students—United States.   4. Master
of business administration degree—United States.   I. Koegler,
Katherine F.   II. Title.

HF1131.M557   3003
658'.0071'1—dc21

                                                    2003044827

D 12 11 10 9 8 7 6 5

Other things may change us,
but we start and end with family.
—*Anthony Brandt*

CONTENTS

Contents

ACKNOWLEDGMENTS

PUBLISHING A BOOK is very much a team effort, and the one you are now holding in your hands would not exist without the hard work, enthusiasm, and devotion of many people working tirelessly behind the scenes who richly deserve to be called into the spotlight to take a bow. First, a CB-Club-level boomalacka to our literary agent, Jake Elwell, for his terrific stewardship of this project, for his constant encouragement, reliable wisdom, and, most of all, his friendship. You could not ask for a steadier hand or a better guide on the long road from the blank page to the finished product.

To our editor, Carolyn Chu, who took over this project in midstream but didn't miss a beat, shepherding it along with patience and enthusiasm, providing the encouragement to keep the pages coming, and making the suggestions to ensure that the finished product "lives up to the hype."

To Kristine Laca at the Tuck School of Business for taking so many hours out of her incredibly busy travel schedule to sit down with us and share such a refreshingly candid look at the admissions process, which, we trust, will bring smiles and comfort to applicants everywhere. Trust us when we tell you: you won't find a more devoted Director of Admissions anywhere.

To Kim Keating at the Tuck School of Business for her generous assistance and enthusiasm, and to Sean Gorman at Sheehan, Phinney, Bass & Green for making the necessary introductions!

To Vernon Loucks, CEO of Segway; Jeff Bezos, CEO of Amazon.com; Ed Whitacre, CEO of SBC; Jim McNerney, CEO of 3M; and Larry Bossidy, CEO of Honeywell, for taking the time away from their management duties to discuss the merits of business school with us, and sharing their valuable insights on when and how going to business school can matter most.

To Charles "Chuck" Knight, chairman and former CEO of Emerson Electric, for honoring us with the contribution of his foreword to this book.

To our outstanding mentoring team: Brett, Amy, Matt, Kanna, Andy, Anne, David, Alden, David, and Toby for finding the time in your busy schedules to animate the pages of this book with your stories and your valuable counsel. We are honored to be associated with all of you for posterity in the pages of this book.

To Christine Aebi, with sincere thanks for your first-rate copy-editing skills.

And, finally, to Carolyn, who greeted us, wide-eyed, with "You're going to do WHAT?!" when we announced our plans to write this book while both of our families were in the process of expansion. Thank you for your support, your love, your encouragement, and for picking up the slack for lo those many months when we retreated to the glow of the midnight oil to advance the cause a few pages further.

FOREWORD

I AM A LONG-TIME SUPPORTER of M.B.A. education. Every year since 1973, Emerson has hired a select group of M.B.A. graduates, some 450 in all. We find they are better prepared every year, and incredibly better prepared than when I earned my M.B.A. more than forty years ago.

Emerson's program has been a great success, in part because we have a simple process for evaluating these young managers. We intentionally put them in jobs they aren't really qualified for—positions where they work with senior people handling real, significant issues. Many rise to the challenge because they see the opportunity for excellent career paths. Remarkably, almost 50 percent of the M.B.A.s we have hired over three decades are still with Emerson. One is David Farr, who joined the company in 1981 and became CEO in 2000. Others include Charles Peters, senior executive vice president, who joined Emerson in 1978, and Walter Galvin, chief financial officer, who joined Emerson thirty years ago after completing his M.B.A. And there are many, many more who play vital roles on the Emerson management team.

Even so, an M.B.A. degree is not a guarantee of success. It is, rather, one ingredient that can make a difference in a career.

I believe sucess in business is related primarily to three things: luck, timing, and leadership. We create our own good luck. Over time, our cumulative actions and efforts enable luck to affect our lives. And as we gain experience and learn about the interaction of complex events, we begin to understand timing, and how to use that understanding to make wise decisions or initiate strategic actions.

Luck and timing are important, but without leadership we may not create the room for good luck, or fully recognize timely opportunities as they unfold over the span of a career. There are many definitions of leadership and many lists of its elements. For purposes of brevity, I suggest that leadership is a tangible way of life—the unique way each of us puts our commitment into action.

For those willing to make the commitment to leadership in business, an M.B.A. program can provide a career edge. Business schools expose us to the powerful presence of leadership or, in some cases, its absence. They pass along valuable accumulated knowledge and experience from one generation to the next. And the relationships formed with classmates and instructors can be lasting and important. I know mine have been.

Business School Confidential is a good tool to begin evaluating whether business school is right for you. If it is, this book will also help you understand how to be admitted, and how to get the most out of this important educational experience. This is a clear and useful guide, and I recommend it highly.

> —Charles F. Knight
> Chairman of Emerson (CEO 1973–2000)
> M.B.A., Cornell University 1959

INTRODUCTION:
HOW TO USE THIS BOOK

"Is there anyone so wise as to learn
by the experience of others?"
— VOLTAIRE

CONGRATULATIONS! By picking up and opening this book, you have just taken the first significant step toward building a productive, successful, and pleasant business school experience. Though you may not know it yet, business school can be an intimidating, foreign, isolating, and competitive place. Sure—at many business schools, you will be assigned a second-year student to serve as your "mentor," and if she isn't too busy with recruiting, her course load, and her extracurricular and social activities, you might be able to glean a few nuggets of wisdom from that relationship. Your school may offer a Dean of Student Affairs, a team of orientation counselors, and a lecture and "math camp" to help you transition from undergraduate life—or, more likely, the working world—into the business school environment. At the end of the day, though, it is going to be just you, alone in professional school, where often it seems that everyone but you knows exactly what he wants and precisely how to accomplish it.

And that's where we, and the rest of your *Business School Confidential* mentors come in.

We can relate, because we've just been there. We've felt that feeling of overwhelming "aloneness" that only the coldly professional business school environment can produce. Collectively we've been caught unprepared by a cold-calling professor, fallen way behind in our reading loads, botched exams, and received some disappointing grades. We've fallen flat on our faces in case interviews, and papered our walls with rejection letters from employers. We've thought about dropping out, wondered why we went to business school in the first place, considered alternate career choices, and anguished over choices of coasts, cities, companies, divisions, and areas of concentration. We've feuded with members of our project groups, and broken up with boyfriends, girlfriends, and spouses who did not understand the commitment that business school entails. We've thrived and stumbled, pulled the all-nighters, blanked out during exams, dealt with difficult employers during summer internships, and locked horns with offensive interviewers during recruiting season.

Despite all of that, we also graduated, got the jobs we wanted, and have successfully moved back out into the business world armed with a degree that makes us more marketable and more valued to our respective employers.

We're not academic professors twenty-five years removed from the business school experience, clueless about the demands of the business world and waxing nostalgic about how wonderful the intellectual side of business can be. We were students just like you, and two short years ago we were where you are now. We know business school is not always a wonderful experience, and that it can be a cold and unwelcome place for the unprepared and the uninitiated.

We're here to give you "the scoop" about business school—the answers to all the stuff that you've always wondered about. If you want the truth about business school—what it's going to take to get in, to get what you want out of it, and to get out with your self-esteem and personality intact—this is the book you want. We expose the traps for the unwary, dispel the mystery, cut through the rhetoric, and simply show you the way to get the utmost out of your business school experience and get out with the job you want.

Simple as that.

In other words, this is a practical, how-to guide to the business school experience. Possessing this book and applying its teachings will give you peace of mind as you move through every aspect of your business school experience. Most of all, it will help you avoid making the same mistakes that we made during the many weeks and months of hard work that lie ahead.

In a moment, we'll be introducing you to your mentoring team—the group of recently graduated students from business schools across the country who will guide you through the next two years with their wisdom and advice culled from personal experience. First, though, a bit of advice about how to get the most out of this book: Whether you are still a college student just starting to think about business school, a working person contemplating going back to get your M.B.A., a student already in business school, or the parent, friend, or significant other of someone in business school trying to understand what your loved one is going through, this book has something to offer you. Determine which of the following sections is most applicable to you, and read accordingly—then meet us on the other side for an introduction to your mentoring team!

I am a college student thinking about applying to business school.

Great! You may have the most to gain from reading this book, since you have the most time to apply our advice and position yourself to maximize your chances for admission to the business school of your choosing.

While it is never too soon to be thinking about business school, the truth is, it may be premature for you to actually apply to business programs straight out of college. Most of the top M.B.A. programs prefer their students to get some post-collegiate work experience prior to applying and attending business school. In fact, the average age of incoming students at the top one hundred graduate business programs is twenty-five.

There are several reasons why business schools prefer applicants who present with actual, real-world business experience. First, a large portion of the academic work in business school is done in groups. In these groups, the different real-world experience each individual brings to the table helps students to learn from one another. Second, it is assumed that incoming business students posses at least some foundational knowledge of business fundamentals—like finance, marketing, and management, and how these areas interact in the real world—a foundation upon which your business school courses will build. If you lack the perspective of having seen business operate from the inside, you will have a much harder time grasping the practical applications of these concepts. Third, it is assumed that students who have been out in the working world have a greater appreciation for, and understanding of, the purpose and need for further education. A student who gives up a well-paying job and accepts the "opportunity cost" that the M.B.A. requires exhibits a clear commitment to the experience and, as such, is likely both to give more to the experience and to get more out of it. Finally, the corporate supporters of the large business schools want the M.B.A. graduates they hire to have some prior real-world experience in addition to their degrees. Since these corporations subsidize a considerable number of students through their financial contributions to the school, they get to weigh in on some of the policymaking decisions at the school. These companies want the graduates they ultimately hire to have as much practical experience as possible because it lowers training costs and smoothes out the learning curve—which is good for their own bottom lines. Business may be many things, but at the end of it all, at least one eye is always on the bottom line.

If you're still in college and are seriously considering business school, you basically have two options. You can, of course, apply directly out of college—but if you choose this route, understand that that you may be significantly limiting the number and types of schools to which you have a realistic chance of admission. Those candidates that are successful in applying to business school directly from college have generally had some exceptional work experience elsewhere—perhaps during the summer, during college, or while growing up. The top-tier schools highly value prior work experience and will favor applicants that present with it. Accordingly, your best option may be to obtain a position in a business-related field that is of interest to you, build some meaningful post-collegiate business experience, perform skillfully, make some connections with people who can function as effective recommenders, and then apply. This is the route chosen by the majority of successful applicants.

Whatever path you choose, this book will help you determine whether business school is right for you now, or might be in the future, and will outline the steps needed to apply, gain admission, and succeed in the program of your choice. So read on!

I am currently working and thinking about applying to business school.

Perfect timing! As previously noted, business schools generally prefer candidates who've obtained at least a couple of years of meaningful work experience in the business world prior to applying to business school. Among the top one hundred schools, the average student has worked for an average of four years prior to matriculating in business school, so if you've worked for at least a couple of years in the business world since graduating from college, obtained some meaningful real-world business experience, and you know why you want an M.B.A., congratulations!—you fit the profile of the primary successful business school applicant.

Given your current position, flip ahead a couple of pages to meet the mentors, then head for the first chapter of this book to determine whether business school is right for you. If you conclude, after reading the first chapter, that business school *is* the way you want to go, this book will then guide you through every facet of the experience—from targeting which programs fit your needs . . . to how to get the most from those programs . . . to financing your education . . . to finding and gaining full-time employment at the firm of your choosing.

I've already been admitted to business school and my program is about to start.

While the material on applying to and choosing a business school program is now moot to you, the rest of this book will give you valuable insight into the demands of business school programs and will provide a wealth of advice about how to excel once you're there! With *Business School Confidential* at your side, you will be fully briefed about the demands of business school and how to meet them, and will learn from the experiences of others, to help you avoid the pitfalls and make the most of your opportunities.

But I'm already in business school . . . I wish I'd found this sooner.

Yeah, we all wish we'd had it sooner, too—but that's why we've written it. Given that you're already down the road a bit, take a peek at the table of contents, jump ahead to where you are in your experience, and go from there. Although every business school is organized differently, this book has been written to correspond at least roughly with the chronological order that most business schools follow. Whether it's your first day on campus or the beginning of your second-year on-campus recruiting season, this book provides the proven advice based on the broad experiences of your just-graduated mentors. Your mentors will address everything from the anxiety of taking their first exam in five years, to choosing a major, to the best methods for preparing for consulting firms' cutthroat case interviews. Armed with this book, you'll always be informed about what lies ahead, and you'll be able to be proactive, rather than reactive, in dealing with the remaining challenges that business school has to offer. It's never too late to learn from the experiences of others!

I'm the parent, friend, sibling, or significant other of someone planning to attend business school.

Business School Confidential is the ideal gift for that special person in your life who is considering or attending business school. Perhaps this person is having trouble determining whether business school is right for them. Perhaps you're wondering what business school is all about, or whether it is even really necessary?

If you know someone thinking about applying to business school, this is the book for them. Written by students, for students, *Business School Confidential* dispels the many mysteries and clears up the confusion about the business school experience, and will help anyone considering attending business school make a better informed choice. Written in plain English and in a conversational style, it will also help *you* better understand the experience, so you can relate to and support your business school student.

* * *

That said, it is now time to meet the mentors who will guide you through the next two years. On the following pages, you can read about their backgrounds, their interests, their professional experience before business school, and their reasons for applying. As you proceed through this book, you'll be able to follow their progress, recognize and learn from their mistakes, and watch their career choices blossom and develop before your eyes. You can and should model some of their actions, choices, strategies, and experiences, and avoid the mistakes they'll tell you about in the pages that follow.

At the end of our business school careers, many of us walked away from the experience shaking our heads and muttering to ourselves, "I wish I knew then what I know now . . ." "If only I had taken . . ." "If I could do this over again, I would . . ." You are in the unique position to have that wish granted.

Let's get started!

The *Business School Confidential* Mentors

BRETT S. RIGGI
New York, New York

B.S.—Yale University (Chemistry and Mathematics), cum laude with distinction
M.B.A.—The Wharton School of the University of Pennsylvania (Finance)

Summer internship: Intel Corporation, Santa Clara, California
Current position: Merrill Lynch—Technology Strategist/Assistant Vice President
Years between college and business school: 6

Job experience before business school: I spent all six years at Merck and Company, Inc., a New Jersey–based pharmaceuticals company. I focused on information technology (IT) for all six years, and in the final five years developed and implemented financial information systems for Merck's international subsidiaries. I had great mentors, and the experience taught me what I would learn in business school, why I needed to learn those things, and how I could leverage my business school education and experiences after earning my M.B.A.

Why I went to business school: During my career at Merck, I learned a good deal about information technology and the basics of management. However, I was developing *financial* information systems and had never taken a course in finance! I loved the subject matter, but felt that my knowledge of the subject matter was weak. Additionally, I aspired (and still aspire!) to become a chief information officer (CIO) for a multinational corporation. To be effective in this capacity, I felt that I needed a management education, the exposure to others with similar interests and ambitions, and the credibility that comes with having an M.B.A. Finally, I sought a change in industry. While Merck has an impeccable reputation as a pharmaceuticals company, I was not passionate about the firm's business. Going to business school, therefore, was a great opportunity for me to learn what else was out there (high-tech, financial services, et cetera), and to make the transition into another industry.

As a college student, I always knew that someday I'd be looking to return to graduate school. My grades, therefore, were important, and I learned how to study in college in a way that ensured I earned solid grades. In business school, by contrast, I worried much less about the grades—they simply didn't matter to anyone but me—and concentrated heavily on learning. Doing so was particularly important for me, as 95 percent of the material taught in classes was brand-new to me. To come out of school a more knowledgeable businessperson, I had to focus on the content being taught, and in retrospect I'm very glad I did.

If I had the choice to make over again, I would go to business school without hesitation.

AMY BELT
New Haven, Connecticut

B.A.—Yale University (Economics)
M.B.A.—The Haas School of Business at the University of California at Berkeley (Strategy and Marketing)

Summer internship: Bristol-Myers Squibb (International Marketing)
Current position: Guidant Corporation—Product Manager/Global Marketing for Angioplasty Systems
Years between college and business school: 5

Job experience before business school: I spent all five years in Healthcare Management Consulting, and worked with hospitals throughout the United States and Canada on strategy, operations, and clinical resource management.

Why I went to business school: I wanted to leave consulting, but my career contacts were limited to other consultants and hospital administrators. From my years of consulting, I knew that I did not want to continue in either consulting or hospital administration at that time. I did not know precisely what I wanted to do, since my exposure, in addition to my network, was limited to those two areas. Business school was an opportunity for me to expand my network, gain exposure to other functions and industries, and build skills that would make me valuable in a new position. I was particularly interested in gaining a firm foundation in finance, accounting, and marketing since I'd had so little chance to build those skills in my consulting work.

The most important thing I learned in business school is that relationships matter.

If I had the choice to make over again, I'd go to business school in a heartbeat.

MATT FATES
Boxford, Massachusetts

B.S.—Yale University (Computer Science and Economics)
M.B.A.—The Tuck School of Business at Dartmouth College (General Management)

Summer internship: Gold Wire Technology—an early-stage software company focused on telecommunications configuration management software
Current position: Ascent Venture Partners (Associate)
Years between college and business school: 4

Job experience before business school: Immediately after college, I joined Alex Brown and Sons, an investment bank focused on small- to mid-sized growth companies. I worked in the technology group within corporate finance. It was a great place to start and I learned a lot, but I eventually determined that I would enjoy working with companies more closely in order to build stronger relationships. I then decided to join Norwest Venture Partners in the Boston office. We invested in early-stage technology companies during the boom years of the Internet—which was amazing, but too good to be true. My boss saw the demise looming and suggested that a few years away from the turmoil would be a good thing. He was right. I applied to B-schools and was fortunate enough to have the privilege of choosing Tuck.

Why I went to business school: I decided to go to business school for a number of reasons. First, it was a good time to take a break from the world of venture capital. Things were about to come crashing down, and my boss was predicting a difficult environment. All the senior partners at the firm I worked for had M.B.A.s, and very highly recommended time spent in business school. At the firm I worked for, no matter how well I did, I could not be promoted without the M.B.A.

I also wanted to build a broader network of people I could learn from, and with whom I could do business. Investing in technology-based companies is still my primary interest, but I know there is a lot more out there in the business world. Finally, I knew it would be fun.

The most important thing I learned in business school is that the experience provides easy access to many people of similar age, with similar interests, who are all smart and motivated. You can learn a lot from these people, build valuable relationships, and really accelerate your career by gaining these contacts, basic business tools, and self-confidence.

If I had the choice to make over again, I would definitely go to business school. I loved my business school experience and feel that it was very worthwhile.

KANNA KUNCHALA
Albany, New York

B.A.—Harvard University (English Literature)
M.B.A.—The Kellogg School of Business at Northwestern University (Finance)

Summer internship: Goldman, Sachs (Equity Sales and trading)
Current position: Goldman, Sachs (Equity Derivatives Sales)
Years between college and business school: 5

Job experience before business school: I spent three years doing community service work for an organization called City Year, and two years as a speechwriter for the City of Boston.

Why I went to business school: I chose to go to business school because my background was in the community and public service sectors, and I thought I needed to get some experience within the corporate sector.

I also planned to spend a few years working outside the government. I knew that a business school degree would make it easier to be "credentialed" in the private sector, and that I would learn the best corporate practices which I could take back with me to the public sector later in my career.

The most important thing I learned in business school is that you will get the most fulfillment from the people you meet and work with. Your fascinating and immensely varied classmates will be the most interesting part of the experience.

ANDY STEWART
Ithaca, New York

B.S.—Cornell University (Hotel Administration/Real Estate and Finance)
M.B.A.—The Wharton School of the University of Pennsylvania (Finance)

Summer internship: Daniels and Associates—a boutique investment banking firm in Denver, Colorado
Current position: Cherokee Investment Partners, LLC (Senior Associate, managing a $600 million real-estate private equity fund)
Years between college and business school: 4

Job experience before business school: After I graduated from Cornell, I joined a real-estate acquisition and development group in Denver, Colorado. I started as the sole acquisition analyst, responsible for processing and analyzing all transactions—single asset and portfolio acquisitions, development deals, et cetera. As the company grew alongside a burgeoning real-estate market, I continued to take on more responsibility, ultimately managing all facets of up to three transactions at any given time. It was a great opportunity for me to learn a lot in a fast-paced, entrepreneurial climate.

Why I went to business school: I periodically evaluate my career and personal objectives. My objective in the early part of my career was to learn as much as possible, surround myself with bright people from whom I could learn, and push myself to the limits in the pursuit of advancement. At the four-year mark, things were changing and, more than ever, I had to reconsider my options. I chose to return to business school for various reasons. First, the situation at my job was not providing a continuous career path and learning curve. I had reached a point where the direction to advance was unclear and uncertain. Part of this was the structure of the organization and the limitations imposed on me, and part was my insatiable appetite to learn and to continue to grow.

Business school was a path to continued personal development. I knew that upon graduation, the degree would mean added credibility. I also felt as though I was pigeonholing my career in real estate, and into one small sector of that industry. I thought it would be prudent to gain exposure to other fields and get a better "macro" understanding of the economy and other business models. There was a lot going on in the economy (the tech boom) that spurred an interest to explore what else was out there. Business school appeared to provide both an opportunity to gain a broader understanding of the macro–business environment and a good platform to launch a career change—if I determined that was something I wanted to do.

ANNE WALKER RUIZ
Bronxville, New York

B.A.—Harvard University (Government)
M.B.A.—Columbia Business School (Finance)

Summer internship: GS.com—marketing for Goldman Sachs' online private wealth management
Current position: Merrill Lynch Equity Capital Markets (Associate)
Years between college and business school: 3

Job experience before business school: I worked on Wall Street in investment banking, spending part of my time in Latin America. I then transferred to a small, regional investment bank in Argentina to get a different experience.

Why I went to business school: I wanted to go to business school to get exposed to more than just finance. I wanted to explore marketing, management, and the various other disciplines while also concentrating on taking advanced finance courses. In addition, as a woman, I thought having the degree would be helpful to give me some added flexibility later in life.

The most important thing I learned in business school is that business is a lot more than just technical skills.

If I had the choice to make over again, I would certainly choose to go to business school.

DAVID LIEBOWICZ
San Francisco, California

B.A—University of California at Berkeley (Integrative Biology)
M.B.A.—The Anderson School at UCLA (International Management)

Summer internship: I accepted an offer from Towers Perrin in their strategic consulting unit. Three days before my start date, all the summer interns and several full-time consultants were laid off due to the downturn in the economy. After scrambling a bit, I ended up consulting for my former employer for a couple of months.

Current position: Guidant Corporation (Product Manager)

Years between college and business school: 6

Job experience before business school: I had always planned on going to medical school. It wasn't until I finished all of the premed course requirements and took the MCAT that I began to question that career route. At graduation from undergrad, I hadn't applied to med school or come up with any alternative career plan, so I decided to use my savings for a trip to Costa Rica. I planned on spending a couple of months relaxing, learning a little Spanish, and finding some inspiration regarding my future. Instead, I found a job as a science teacher at a private American high school and stayed a year. The next year, still without inspiration but with a strong desire to keep traveling, I volunteered for a Peace Corps–like program in Israel and spent a year there. Following the Israel program, I returned home and found a job as a pharmaceutical sales rep in San Francisco. After a year and a half in the field, I took a job in business development at a pharmaceutical startup in Palo Alto, where I worked for two and a half years before starting business school.

Why I went to business school: I went to business school for three primary reasons. First was the effect the degree would have on my long-term competitiveness in the marketplace. Most American companies seem to like, if not require, an M.B.A. in order to ascend to senior management. Second, I felt I could use the education. I didn't know enough about valuation, finance, or accounting to do my job as well as I would have liked. I was constantly trying to learn this stuff on the fly, and it always seemed like an uphill battle. Finally, all of the M.B.A.s I spoke with had a great time in school, learned a ton, and made a lot more money after they graduated. So it sounded like a great deal!

ALDEN M. WHITTAKER
Denver, Colorado

B.A.—Middlebury College (Environmental Studies)
M.E.S.—Yale School of Forestry and Environmental Studies (Environmental Studies)
M.P.P.M.—Yale School of Management (Nonprofit Management)

Summer internship: Great Outdoors Colorado—Denver, Colorado
Current position: Denver Water Department (Real Estate analyst)
Years between college and business school: 3

Job experience before business school: I worked for a series of environmental nonprofits. I started with the Peregrine Fund in Boise, Idaho, where I camped for two months on top of a ridge in the Wenachee National Forest in central Washington feeding six captive-bred Peregrine Falcons, observing their flying and hunting behavior until they were self-sufficient. I then joined the Help Our Wildlife Rehabilitation Center outside Seattle, Washington, where I helped to rehabilitate injured and orphaned wildlife. I moved to Naples, Florida, and worked at the Conservancy Nature Center managing ten years of research data on sea turtles. I worked as a wildlife research assistant for the Yellowstone Project in Yellowstone National Park, Wyoming, assisting Ph.D. students with data collection on a coyote behavior study, and led a public program to research small mammal populations. I then worked for the Idaho Department of Fish and Game doing surveys and analyzing data. Finally, I moved to New York and worked for the American International Group (AIG) helping the training personnel in the accounting department use a custom-designed software program.

Why I went to business school: I knew I eventually wanted to work for an environmental nonprofit organization. I had heard and seen that nonprofits in this area are generally not very well run because it is often people with the passion and the field experience who assume management positions. I wanted to gain good management skills and bring them to the environmental nonprofit arena.

I learned the most in business school from exposure to the many different aspects of business in the private sector that I had previously known very little about: statistics, economics, marketing, decision-making, finance, politics, investing, quality control, manufacturing, organizational behavior, competitive strategy, negotiation, operations, leadership, teamwork, accounting, taxes, financial statement analysis, technological innovation, and on and on. I don't expect to use all of the knowledge that I gained in these classes in the everyday world of my career, but such knowledge allows me to understand the world around me, both in and out of the work environment, much more keenly.

If I had it to do over again, I wouldn't change a thing.

DAVID ("DAVE") BUSSA
Madison, Wisconsin

B.A.—University of Wisconsin–Madison (**Advertising and Communications**)

I.M.B.A.—The Daniels College of Business at the University of Denver (Financing and Marketing of New Ventures)

Summer internship: I went to school year-round
Current position: Undecided
Years between college and business school: 5

Job experience before business school: I was the International Marketing and Sales Management for a diagnostic cardiology manufacturer.

Why I went to business school: The position I held before going to business school exposed me to all aspects of our company. I saw the importance of having all business units within a company functioning together; however, my lack of a formal business education made it difficult for me to understand the details associated with running each business unit. My desire is to "run the show" someday. You do not need to be an expert in each area of a business to be a CEO, but you need to know what makes each unit successful, and you need to know what options are available to make each unit run efficiently. The M.B.A.— or in my case, the I.M.B.A.—educates you about the options, teaches you how to deal with common personnel issues, and trains you on what is required to install an effective business strategy.

TOBY D. STICKLER
New York, New York

B.S.—New York University Stern School of Business (Finance and Marketing)

M.B.A.—The Wharton School of the University of Pennsylvania (Strategic Management and Information Systems Strategy and Economics)

Summer internship: Bain and Company, Inc.—Boston
Current position: Bain and Company, Inc.—New York (Consultant)
Years between college and business school: 3

Job experience before business school: As an analyst in Andersen Consulting's (now Accenture) Process Competency Group, I gained invaluable exposure to a broad array of clients within the financial services industry. My daily work at Andersen provided me with deep functional skills, with a strong emphasis on technology. In addition, I learned to effectively manage client demands and project deadlines and had the opportunity to assume different positions within a team structure. I realized, however, that I was most interested in studying an organization as a whole and understanding the business need for the changes we implemented. As such, I concluded that I wanted to pursue a career in strategy consulting, and that an M.B.A. would be critical in effecting this career switch.

I also realized, however, that before returning to school, I would need to obtain more significant managerial experience and assume a position where I could devise and implement my own ideas. I was seeking a "bridge job"—one that would enable me to build on skills that I had already acquired while acquainting me with the strategy experience I was seeking. Thus, after one and a half years, I left Andersen Consulting and joined American Express as an internal consultant and liaison between the Technologies Department and the Relationship Services business unit. In this capacity, I was involved in all aspects of new product development, ranging from up-front business planning to systems implementation. I was also responsible for supervising my team, handling group communications, and working with the CFO to track budget expenditures. After eighteen months at American Express, I left to go to business school.

Why I went to business school: Prior to business school, I worked for three years in a technology development and project management capacity. I was more interested, however, in the business rationale behind the systems changes I was responsible for. I knew that I wanted to transition into a strategy role. In order to make that career move, however, I felt that getting an M.B.A. was necessary.

1

So You Wanna Get an M.B.A.

"Know the right moment."
— THE SEVEN SAGES

IT PROBABLY COMES as no surprise to you that pursuing a master's degree is an expensive and time-consuming proposition. Leaving a solid, well-paying job to pursue an M.B.A. should be a carefully considered and calculated decision. Before committing two years of your life; at least $60,000 in tuition, fees, and housing; and the "opportunity cost" of the experience—ask yourself the following questions and force yourself to really think through your honest responses to them. It may help to actually write your answers down. Taking the time to do this will make it easier to carefully and properly evaluate business school as a next step in your career.

Why do I really want to go to business school?

There are many possible responses to this question, and most business school applicants actually have more than one. Many of these reasons are well thought-out and will empower your experience. Others, however, should not be the premise upon which you decide to apply.

"I think deciding whether or not to go to business school is a matter of figuring out where your interests lie," Dave notes. "If you are happy working in the accounting sector or the marketing sector and have no desire to cross over into other areas in the future, then you may not need to go to business school. If you want to explore new areas of business, grow your understanding of how business works, and give yourself the option of moving around in the future, then you should give serious thought to business school."

Andy agrees. "I would encourage anyone thinking about applying to business school to carefully evaluate their career objectives. The fact of the matter is that too many people have a great deal of uncertainty about that. The most important step is to figure out what it is that you really want to do, and to do that *before* you apply."

"When I first applied to Wharton in 1996, I had *no idea* what I was looking to get out of my business school education. I could not articulate the value that an M.B.A. would have for me. It was only the second time around, after a great deal of independent research and countless conversations with other business school graduates that I appreciated why it was that I wanted to go to business school," Brett admits. "You want to be able to look at your career to date, and specify exactly how getting an M.B.A. will help you grow, both professionally and personally."

Okay. So this is the time of reckoning. Check to see if one or more of your reasons for applying to business school appears on this list:

- I kicked ass on the GMAT—I can't ignore that, can I?
- I hate my job, so this will be my "way out."
- The economy stinks, and I just got laid off, so why not go back to school?
- This is what all my friends are doing—they can't all be wrong . . .

- Everyone else in my firm has an M.B.A.
- I don't understand science, so med school is out, and law school requires too much reading. What else is there?

If your primary reason for applying to business school is represented by one or any combination of the responses from the list above—slam on the brakes! It's time to spend some more time considering your motivations. Follow along, and you'll see why.

I kicked ass on the GMAT—I can't ignore that, can I?

Uh . . . yeah. You can . . . and if crushing the GMAT is your best reason for applying to business school, you probably should!

While you are to be congratulated for acing this important test, the only thing the GMAT measures with certainty is how well you did on a certain set of computerized questions on one given day.

That's it.

The Educational Testing Service (ETS) would have you believe that there is a strong correlation between an individual's performance on the GMAT and his success in business school and in business in general, but this claim is certainly not without controversy. Doing well on the GMAT is not a guarantee that you will do well in business school and, more importantly, it says nothing about whether you are well suited for business school, will enjoy business school, or actually need the degree. There are many successful CEOs, financiers, and entrepreneurs who never set foot in a business school classroom. You need a better reason than a good score on a standardized exam to make this level of commitment. View a good GMAT score simply as an element of your application—not as the justification for it.

A good GMAT score may get you into the dance, but it's no guarantee you'll be happy to be there. Force yourself to look deeper for a better motivation.

I hate my job, so this will be my "way out."

Okay . . . so you'd be willing to pay a headhunter $80,000 and give him two years of your life in exchange for a new job, right?

No?

Then why would you pay the lofty price of attending business school just to get out of your present employment situation? This is pure laziness. If you hate your job, contact a headhunter, search the classifieds, or hop on the Internet and cruise the myriad employment sites offered there *for free*. Applying to business school—or any graduate program, for that matter—because you hate your current job and have no idea what you really want to do with your life, is a recipe for disappointment.

Why?

Because with no idea why you want to go to business school, you'll have a difficult time making a convincing case for yourself in your admissions essays and interviews, which may lead to rejection after rejection, and a waste of the time and money associated with applying. If do you happen to fool somebody into offering you admission, however, when you get to business school, you'll still have no idea why you are there—no particular focus, no direction, and no passion fueling your study. Sure, you might find your passion while you are there, but you are just as likely not to. Know where you'll be then?

Right back where you started. Frustrated, without direction, resentful of your employment situation . . . $80,000 in debt, and two years older.

Read on.

The economy stinks, and I just got laid off, so why not go back to school?

So you got laid off and the economy is in recession. In the year 2001, a record number of people applied to business school as a result of layoffs and the downturn in the economy. A popular rumor that year had it that one out of every five pieces of mail coming out of Silicon Valley post offices was a business school application.

If your employment status and the economy are your primary motivations for applying to business school, you are not alone. Recognize, however, that these are not the kinds of motivations likely to impress admissions committees inundated with applications from thousands of candidates in the same position. Not to mention the fact that your chances of admission are significantly decreased due to the increased number of applications!

Finally, you should also be aware that simply having an M.B.A. is not a guaranteed ticket to a well-paying job after graduation. If the economy hasn't improved by the time you graduate, you could still be without a job—with the additional burden of your student loans. Many members of the business school classes of 2001 had their employment offers *rescinded* because of economic factors, and countless others had their start dates pushed back by many months.

Don't use business school as a backup plan.

This is what all my friends are doing—they can't all be wrong . . .

Known to past generations as the Brooklyn Bridge theorem. You know, the one your mother always used to rebut this reasoning. "If all of your friends were going to jump off the Brooklyn Bridge . . ."

Forget what all your friends are doing. Your friends may have very good reasons for applying to business school, or may have absolutely no clue why they are doing so. Either way, unless their reasons apply directly to you—what your friends are doing should have no impact on your decision. Don't be a lemming. Your friends won't be ponying up the monthly debt service payments on your student loans for the next ten years, so don't let them decide whether you should go to business·school.

Everyone else in my firm has an M.B.A.

This might be a good reason to go to business school—if you have long-term intentions to stay at your current place of employment, and if your superiors have indicated to you that an M.B.A. would help you advance. Some companies do impose a sort of "glass ceiling" which, at some point, can stop people without M.B.A.s from further ascension through the ranks. But before you start completing those applications, sit back and ask yourself the hard questions. What do you hope to get out of business school, and what will be the "opportunity cost" of two years away from the working world? Finally, before you leave the working world for business school with only a year or two of real-world experience, consider the fact that when you graduate, prospective employers, including the company you left, may look at you as an inexperienced, overeducated prospective employee with a high price tag.

Not necessarily a recipe for success.

If you leave your company to go to business school for the aforementioned reason, be relatively certain that you'd like to work there long-term, and get some assurances that the company actually wants *you* to work there long-term. And finally, be aware that in the two years you are away, economic factors can change that could wholly change these circumstances.

The bottom line is, it is generally best not to go to business school unless it is actually something *you* want to do for yourself.

I don't understand science, so med school is out, and law school requires too much reading. What else is there?

And the only other option in the world is to apply to business school? Come on, think a little harder.

The world is full of interesting opportunities. Don't default into applying to business school just because you feel you need a graduate degree, don't want to do medical school or law school, and can't come up with another alternative. The decision to go to business school should not be based solely on the things you know you *don't* want to do. Even if you managed to get admitted with this flimsy rationale, passion won't be driving your experience, and as a result, the experience won't be nearly as enjoyable or fulfilling. Make the decision to pursue an M.B.A. based on your long-term goals, and the specific skills and knowledge you want to gain that will help you reach those goals.

"Some people have told me that they pursued their M.B.A.s for personal reasons, to help them better understand the stock market and how to manage their own investments. Can you believe that? Business school is too time-consuming and too expensive to undertake for something you could get with a subscription to the *Wall Street Journal* and a library card!" Dave warns.

Even if you have figured out that you are interested in business, it does not necessarily mean that going to business school is the right choice. "Business school is definitely not for everyone," David cautions. "The two most successful young entrepreneurs I know wouldn't do well in an M.B.A. program. Given their natural business sense and insane productivity, they probably would have problems with the pace and find it to be a waste of time."

* * *

"All right, all right," you're saying. "Enough gloom and doom, and enough lecturing about why I shouldn't go to business school." Assuming you have navigated the above rationale no-nos and know that none of those reasons is your impetus for going to business school—how do you actually figure out whether business school is *right* for you?

Ah . . . Read on.

A Realistic Evaluation of Your Readiness for Business School

Go somewhere where you can be undisturbed for the next thirty minutes or so and force yourself to answer this next set of questions honestly. Turn off the TV, turn off your cell phone, and concentrate—because in the next couple of pages, we're going to figure out whether you should apply to business school or not. "You need to decide what it is you want to do, what skills you'll need to get there, what skills you'll need to be effective once you do get there, and then determine whether the skills you need are skills best gained in the business school arena," Alden explains.

"And you need to do that *before* you apply," Andy insists.

So don't just passively read these questions and plow forward. Force yourself to engage them, and reflect on the real answers that come from your heart and your gut. You paid good money for this book. Use it! This might be the most valuable exercise you undertake during this entire process.

- What exactly do you want to do with your M.B.A. once you have it?

- Can you accomplish those career goals without an M.B.A. or is the degree viewed as a rite of passage that will accelerate your promotion track and help you penetrate upper management?
- Will an M.B.A. increase your perceived value by employers? How have you determined this?
- Will an M.B.A. enable you to earn a higher salary in your field of interest? How have you determined this?
- Have you asked anyone in your primary field of interest these questions? Did their answers definitively support your going to business school?
- What do you hope to get out of your time in business school?
- What disciplines do you want to focus on? Finance? Marketing? Nonprofit management? Entrepreneurship? Negotiation? Why? How will these skills help advance your career goals?

Don't know the answers to one or more of these questions? That's okay—a lot of us didn't . . . but this is one of the lessons we learned: Do your homework up front so you know exactly why you are applying to business school and what you want to get out of it. The ability to really hone in and focus on your career goals during business school will give you real power. Before you apply to business school, research the answers to these questions, and have a clear answer for each one. You'll be glad you did.

Now ask yourself this second set of questions, which has more to do with the everyday experience of business school:

- Are you self-reliant, or do you depend on others for constant encouragement, evaluation, and/or affirmation?
- Are you comfortable with, and do you enjoy working with, people of varied backgrounds and skill sets?

- Can you seize the main points of an assignment and move on, or do you typically get bogged down in minute details?
- Are you comfortable speaking out in front of a group and arguing your positions in front of others?
- Do you like to think creatively?
- Are you disciplined enough to get up and attend classes on a daily basis?
- Are you prepared to sacrifice most weekday evenings to assignments, and many weekends to group meetings, projects, and other school-related activities?
- Are you adept at, and do you enjoy, managing several tasks simultaneously?
- Are you a go-getter? Is your personality more proactive than reactive?
- Are you 100 percent committed to business school, or do you have several other hobbies and interests competing for your time?

Time Commitment

Business school is extraordinarily time-consuming. Between classes, reading assignments, case preparation, groupwork, extracurricular activities and events, exam preparation, and job hunting, very little of your time during at least the first year and a half will be your own. The typical business school day begins at eight or nine in the morning and frequently ends with a group project or class preparation that will take you well into the evening hours. Don't expect business school to be a "nine-to-five" kind of experience, and don't plan to see a lot of your spouse or children during the experience. Business school is a full-time commitment. Thinking you can make it otherwise is a fool's folly. Forewarned is forearmed.

Teamwork

Business school is a graduate preparatory program for future business managers. As such, business school involves a lot of group work to train students for their future roles dealing with project team members, superiors, and subordinates.

Often, especially in the first term, group members will be assigned, rather than selected. Nonvoluntary group assignment is an effort to get students of different vocational, cultural, and ethnic backgrounds to learn to work with each other. It is not always easy, but working through such vocational, cultural, and ethnic differences and biases can be eye-opening and immensely rewarding, and provides excellent training and preparation for a business career.

Group work requires students to divide labor, assign responsibilities, and depend on each other. It also helps students learn, sometimes the hard way, the importance of supporting and strengthening the weakest link in order to allow the group to prosper as a whole. You must be willing to both lead and follow, talk and listen, carry out your own responsibilities and teach others. At some point, everyone is the weakest link on a project. The group experience—both giving and receiving—can teach you a lot.

The Necessity of Multitasking

In addition to teaching students to become better managers of people, business school trains students to be able to manage several different tasks at once. Most business school students take at least four classes each term, are involved in several nonacademic groups, clubs, or other extracurricular activities, and are constantly networking, job hunting, or going on interviews and callbacks. Among all of these commitments, you will frequently find yourself with a dozen or more projects, responsibilities, and deadlines to manage at the same time. And you don't have a personal assistant to help keep it all straight! If being organized (or at least learning to be organized) and managing several areas—including your academic life, your prospective future in the working world, and your commitment to others—at the same time does not sound like your bag, you might want to reconsider a career in business.

Competition

However subtle it may be, in business school, nearly everyone is looking out for Number One. It may sound harsh and even like a contradiction, given all the groupwork and encouragement to collaborate with your classmates, but at the end of the day, business school is, after all, professional school—and everyone has her own agenda to further.

Competition at most business schools is keen both inside and outside the classroom. Most schools operate on a strict grading curve, mandating that a certain percent of As, Bs, Cs, and Fs be distributed in each class. The lowest grades (that's an F to you and me, folks) are routinely given, and some schools even mandate that the lowest 10 percent of each course be failed to "separate the wheat from the chaff." This does make grades a zero-sum game in business school—and, as you might expect, that can foster serious competition between students.

While competition in the classroom is tough, the more overt battles are waged during recruiting season. During recruiting season, there are appearances at company recruiting events, networking opportunities with alumni, and round after round of competitive interviewing. Students vie with each other to attend the most recruiting events (some of which are by invitation only), to meet the largest number of potential employers, and to be invited to the largest number of "closed" interviews (granted by invitation only and discussed at length in later chapters).

Recruiting season is dealt with twice in this book—for first-year students, and again for second-year students—and those chapters treat extensively with how to navigate the unpleasantness that often arises out of this season of open competition among friends and classmates. Suffice it to say, for now, that if you can't stomach overt competition for grades and jobs, you may want to reconsider your consideration of business school, and a career in business in general.

Conclusion

Figured it out yet?

Hopefully, this chapter has forced you into some serious introspection, and with any luck, that process has either convinced you that you are *not* ready to go to business school, or has helped to crystallize the reasons why business school is the right move for you at this point in your life.

But what if, after all of that, you're still not sure?

Read on. We think the next chapter will help a lot. Once you've finished reading it, come back and reread this chapter again.

2

Taking It to the Top:
Advice from Five Top CEOs About
How to Determine When, and *If,*
Business School Is Right for You

"There is a tide in the affairs of men,
which, taken at the flood,
leads on to fortune."
— WILLIAM SHAKESPEARE

IF YOU READ the first chapter carefully, you should already have a pretty good idea about whether business school is a good match for your present station in life. You've considered the questions we laid out for you, met the mentoring team and examined their diverse and varied paths to business school, and, hopefully, you've begun to think critically about whether now, or any time, is a good time for you to make the turn onto the road to business school yourself.

And no doubt there are at least some of you who skimmed through that first chapter with a "Yeah, yeah . . . just tell me what it's all about" and a wave of the hand.

For you, and everyone else on the fence, we now bring out the big guns.

It's not every day you have five of the nation's top CEOs assembled to speak to your questions about business school. So take a deep breath, take a seat, slow down, and digest. It's time to hear from the bosses.

THE CEO ROUNDTABLE

Jeffrey P. Bezos, chairman and CEO of Amazon.com, Inc.

Lawrence A. Bossidy, former chairman and CEO of Honeywell International Inc.

Vernon R. Loucks, Jr., CEO of Segway LLC and former chairman and CEO of Baxter International

W. James McNerney, Jr., chairman and CEO of The 3M Company

Edward E. Whitacre, Jr., chairman and CEO of SBC Communications, Inc.

So the first question is, what value does an M.B.A. really have in your eyes? Do you feel that having an M.B.A. on your résumé really makes a difference in the business world, and do you feel that there is a perceptible difference in the individuals at your company with M.B.A. degrees versus those without them?

Mr. Bezos: An M.B.A. can help people develop flexible and well-rounded skill-sets and can help teach individuals how to think strategically. It provides unusual perspective across a lot of businesses and industries. We value M.B.A.s who are critical, analytical thinkers who can play diverse roles in our organization. That said, I don't think the degree, by itself, is the key. The degree prepares people and opens some doors, but it's what the individual does with the degree that makes a difference. We have superstars at our company who have an M.B.A. and many who do not. The question is how people apply their skills.

Mr. Whitacre: Yeah, our basic philosophy at SBC is to simply hire good people, and to give them opportunities to perform different jobs, have different experiences, and hope that we can continue to challenge that individual throughout his career. We do tend to hire M.B.A.s into two areas. First, we hire M.B.A.s into something we call our "high potential hire" program that is designed to produce the future leaders of the business ten or fifteen years down the road. And we also hire M.B.A.s in special areas like finance, strategic planning, and mergers and acquisitions. But we also hire non-M.B.A.s into all of those positions, and to be honest, you can't always tell much difference between them! Some of the skills coming right out of school, particularly in finance, are helpful to have. The financial knowledge and skill set that M.B.A.s come in with are very helpful. Those things can be learned on the job, but it's a steep learning curve.

So what are the benefits of going to business school and getting the M.B.A., then?

Mr. Loucks: The value is not in having the M.B.A. on your résumé. The value is in the skills you bring to the table with you after business school. You definitely learn valuable skills in business school, and business school condenses that learning into a short period of time and covers a broad array of topics that would take you much longer to learn and master if you had to learn all of it on the job. M.B.A. graduates are certainly worth the additional expense if you know how to use their talents—but you have to know what you're getting and how to tap into those skills. Over the years, I have found that you can give M.B.A. graduates a lot of independence and have confidence that they will get things done. It is much more of a risk doing that with someone with only a general background who might not have the necessary skills to respond. With M.B.A. grads, there is a baseline of knowledge you can count on.

Mr. Bossidy: In my view, an M.B.A. degree is a good credential that can be helpful to you early in your career. It communicates to people that you've cleared a significant screen. Business school provides you with a broad, rounded education, provides you with a broader perspective than you would get otherwise, and allows you to progress quickly in your ability to perform, understand, and achieve a comfort level with various types of quantitative analysis.

Mr. McNerney: Right—business school accelerates and concentrates one's learning of the mechanics of business. You can learn those things on the job, it just takes much longer to get up to speed. Going to business school also puts you in day-to-day contact with students who are highly qualified, bright, and ambitious, which can really help you realize what a higher standard is. Students in business school really push each other, and that kind of serious competition is excellent preparation for the real world. I also think that there are certain areas like consulting, brand management, or, in high level management positions where having an M.B.A. is especially useful. But there are other, more purely leadership roles like sales leadership positions or factory management positions where leadership is at a premium but sophisticated business tools are not used very often where it is arguable whether you really need an M.B.A.

Mr. Bossidy: On the other hand, people with M.B.A.s are not always as patient as they need to be. Simply getting the credential does not mean that you are ready to run the company! I find that occasionally, people with M.B.A.s can be a little overconfident sometimes, and they can be a higher risk to hire because they can be very impatient and inclined to test the market when they don't experience rapid ascension through the ranks of the company.

Do the U.S. News & World Report, Business Week, *and* Wall Street Journal *rankings influence which schools your company recruits at? How much validity do you place on these rankings?*

Mr. Bezos: We don't use these rankings much at Amazon.com, but my guess is they have some validity; whether it's as much as people give them credit for, I just don't know. We have a group of top business schools that we actively recruit from that's driven mostly by where we've had successful alumni. That's how we rank schools—the success that their alumni have had at Amazon.com. That works out really well.

Mr. McNerney: Well, I'd say that the rankings provide useful information, but they do not define our hiring process. I think the first and second tiers of schools as groups are generally accurate, but I'm not sure I'd pay too much attention to the specific rankings within those tiers. One of the things we do look at is the employers column—have other employers found students from the particular program to be valuable leaders in their companies? We also focus on student engagement in the programs—how much energy and enthusiasm we see in the student body. 3M recruits on a national basis, but we also work with the nearby programs. Local affiliation is very important, and we work very hard with the local schools to help them improve their programs.

Mr. Loucks: Yeah, I think the precise rankings are to be debated since each publication comes out with different placements depending on the exact criteria used, but I think the top ten or so schools, as a group, are accurate, and if you can get into and do well at one of these schools, it's nirvana.

Mr. Whitacre: Our studies have shown that most people wind up one hundred miles or so from where they went to school, so at SBC, we tend to hire more based on geography than on the particular school someone went to. It seems to work well for us. Candidates from nearby schools tend to know our company, but I guess we are fortunate to operate in places where there are some really good business schools.

But with respect to the applications that might come in from more distant places from people who are interested in your company but may not be in your area, does the rank of the school they're coming from play any role in your company's decisions about hiring?

Mr. Whitacre: I hate to say it doesn't play any role, but it doesn't play a very big role. We recruit individuals, we don't recruit degree plans. We don't believe that having an M.B.A. from a top school gives anyone an entitlement. Don't get me wrong, it's important. Having an M.B.A. from a top school is important—but only if the individual who has the degree can otherwise demonstrate that he or she can be effective at SBC.

Okay, so we've heard that the rankings are helpful at least to break the schools into tiers, and to the extent that they measure employer satisfaction with alums of particular schools, and we've heard about the importance of local programs. Is there a cutoff point, in your minds, where getting an M.B.A. from a lesser ranked program is not worth it?

Mr. Loucks: Yes. Some schools are simply not worth the opportunity cost to your career. In some cases, it could be because the program just isn't that good. You need to do your own research about that. One of the ways you can determine that is by which companies are hiring grads from a particular school. If the school isn't getting the kind of attention from the companies you'd hope to work for, it's probably best for you to stand pat where you are.

Mr. Bossidy: The benefits of going to a top program are the networking opportunities and the ability to associate with top faculty and classmates. If you can't get into one of the top twenty or so programs, or a program that you know is especially well suited to your particular circumstances, I'm not sure I think it's worth it to go to business school.

Is there a particular kind of work experience that you like your M.B.A graduates to have prior to going to business school? Do you tend to prefer the entrepreneur over the consultant or investment banker or vice-versa?

Mr. Bezos: There isn't one type of experience we're looking for prior to business school. We definitely want people who—no matter what they did—showed that they're very quantitative and analytical. It's great if they have some background with computer science, technology, or at least with innovation. Consumer-oriented experience is helpful. It's a big plus if they're entrepreneurial and comfortable in fast-paced, dynamic envioronments. It's essential that they're tenacious and willing to roll up their sleeves to do what it takes to get it right for customers. They must have high standards and be team players. But, above all else, the most successful people at Amazon.com are passionate about customer experience, innovating on behalf of customers, and fluent with technology.

Mr. Loucks: No, just that it is better to have some experience than not. At the time I went to business school, the majority of people went directly from college, but I'm sure I would have gotten much more out of the experience if I had worked prior to going. Doing so will give you a much better idea of what you want to do long-term and how you plan to use your M.B.A. to get you there.

Last question to all of you. If your own son or daughter was thinking about applying to business school, what advice would you give to him or her based on all of the experiences you have gathered throughout your careers?

Mr. Bezos: Remember, I don't have an M.B.A., so I only speak from what I've observed. But I'd ask my son or daughter why they want to go. And I'd push them to be very clear about what their expectations are. Often, and at a business like ours, you don't need an M.B.A. to succeed. So getting the degree for the sake of having the credential is not reason enough, in my opinion. But if you want to round out your skill-set (either in areas you're interested in or feel weak about), or reset your career direction a little bit, an M.B.A. is a fantastic way to do it.

Mr. McNerney: I would encourage them to go to business school and to try to get into a top school, but I would also remind them that business school is not really capable of teaching leadership. Leadership is talked about in business school, but it is really best learned on the job. You can really only learn leadership, ethics, and integrity in the pressure of the real world. And finally, that in the business world, how you do something is sometimes even more important that what you do.

Mr. Bossidy: Work for a few years before you apply, to broaden your perspective and make you a more mature participant in the classroom, and to tether the business school experience back to how you will implement it in the real world. And then, when you're ready, get into the most reputable school you can for what it is you want to do.

Mr. Whitacre: Make sure you're going for the right reason—to round out your experience, your knowledge, your skills, and to make you more competitive and more effective—but don't get the M.B.A. just because you think it entitles you to a big salary, because that's not what the degree is for. The M.B.A. only makes a difference if the person behind it can demonstrate effectiveness.

Mr. Loucks: Know why it is that you want to go, and how you plan to use your M.B.A. when you get out. While you're in business school, pay serious respect to your study groups. Your participation in these groups is very similar to running a business. There's a collection of expertise all working together to accomplish one thing—which is a minimodel of a business. And enjoy the experience!

3

Beating the GMAT

"Training is everything."
— MARK TWAIN

UNFORTUNATELY, THERE IS just no getting around it: If you want to go to business school, sooner or later, you're going to have to take the GMAT, as this standardized admissions test is a requirement at nearly all accredited business schools in the United States.

For those of you who are natural-born standardized-test–takers, overcoming the GMAT may not present much of a problem. For the rest of us, however, taking the first sample test will quickly display just how much room there is for improvement! As with all standardized tests, however, this exam can be studied for and beaten. Doing so, however, will take preparation—and preparing adequately for the GMAT is critical.

SO WHAT IS THE GMAT, ANYWAY?

The Graduate Management Admission Test (GMAT) is a standardized test created by the Educational Testing Service (ETS)—the same nice folks who brought you the PSAT and the SAT, and who foist the MCAT and LSAT on your friends. Three and a half hours in length, the test is ostensibly designed to measure your verbal and math skills. It has been likened by some to a "souped-up" SAT because, like the SAT, it is composed of verbal and math sections.

The verbal section of the exam is comprised of multiple-choice questions in three subject areas, including (1) reading comprehension, (2) logical reasoning, and (3) grammar and usage. The math section of the exam also poses three types of multiple-choice questions, in (1) basic arithmetic, (2) algebra, and (3) geometry. The test also features something called an "Analytical Writing Assessment," which in plain English translates into two 30-minute essays.

Until October 1997, the GMAT was administered in writing, and was only offered a few times a year to hundreds of anxious students at once, packed like sardines into gymnasiums or tiny classrooms across the country on the designated days. Thanks to advanced technology, however, today the GMAT is offered on an almost daily basis and is administered exclusively in a computerized format known as the Computer Adaptive Test. The test is "smart"—in that, unlike its paper ancestors, it actually keys in to your performance as you proceed through a series of questions and selects the difficulty of forthcoming questions based on your answers to previous questions.

Lost?

Already yearning for ovals and a number 2 pencil?

Yeah, we were, too, at first. But hang with us for a minute as we illustrate with an example.

Each section of the test begins with a question of moderate difficulty. A correct response will produce a question of increased difficulty, while an incorrect response will produce an easier question. Questions at the beginning of each section have a greater impact on your overall score than questions late in a section, because your correct (or incorrect) responses to early questions produce much more significant distinctions than do later questions. Careless errors, or errors caused by guessing on easy or moderately difficult early questions, can crater your overall score. As such, it is critical to spend the time it takes to get the early questions correct. This can be extremely unnerving, because you may begin paying attention to the perceived difficulty of the questions you are getting, rather than concentrating on their content and getting the right answer.

It is also important to remember that, as with all other standardized tests, the GMAT includes an entire set of "experimental" questions being tested for future use that do not count toward your score. These questions are distributed randomly and, since their difficulty level has not yet been properly gauged, experimental questions are not keyed to the difficulty of the questions you answered previously. Since you never know which questions are experimental, the appearance of an apparently easy question, midexam, is not necessarily indicative of your having answered a series of previous questions incorrectly. Stay focused on the content of each individual question and don't try to determine how well you are doing.

When you have completed the predetermined number of questions in each section, your score is calculated based on how many questions you answered correctly *and* on the difficulty level of those questions. Thus it is possible for two people to answer the same number of questions correctly but to end up with vastly different scores.

Got it?

"It's all about pace," Brett notes. "Going into the exam, you know exactly how many verbal and how many quantitative questions you will be given. You'll also know how much time you have to complete each section. Plan accordingly, and don't let yourself fall behind. If you're nervous before the test begins, warm up with the writing assessment, which will take you through the first hour of the exam. Use that hour to get loose and into the test-taking groove."

Another major change from the standardized test of old—and from the strategies of old as well—is that you can no longer skip over tough questions and come back to them at the end. With the new computerized format, there is no going back. Once you have answered a question and moved on to the next question, you cannot go back to review or alter your answers to any of the previous questions. After years of being taught to "skip the hard questions and come back to them if you have time," this change can be very unnerving to the untrained test-taker. The finality on any given question is hard to deal with, especially when you encounter a question that you can narrow only to a 50-50 guess, or worse. This, however, is where training with practice tests can really help boost your confidence. Gaining a measure of comfort in making choices quickly and definitively, and learning to recognize question types and the tricks embedded in them, can dramatically improve your overall exam performance.

"The year I took the GMAT was the first year it was administered on the computer, and boy, was it different! The atmosphere in the waiting room at the testing center was like a doctor's office—sterile and silent, everyone avoiding eye contact with each other and staring apprehensively at the closed door to the testing room. I could sense this overwhelming feeling of anxiety from the other five people in the room with me who had appointments at the same time. Eventually a woman opened the door and led us into a control room with computers and a big glass wall looking out on the testing room. One by one, we were admitted into the control room, asked for our two sources of identification, asked to sign in, and led to a specific computer terminal in the testing room where our die would be cast . . . Six pathetic souls in a ten- by ten-foot testing room, trying to overcome the one last standardized test that held the key to our futures in graduate school."

—Katherine

"The computerized test format can be very foreign to people, so taking sample tests in the medium in which they are administered in definitely an advantage," Amy suggests.

"Practice, practice, practice! The material actually tested on the GMAT is not terribly difficult, but it does require that you learn *how* to take the test. There are different strategies for different portions of the exam. You need to learn to recognize what is being tested, how to approach the questions, and how to answer the questions as quickly as possible, and you need to get used to taking the exams on a computer," Toby adds.

Canceling Your Score

Oh, there is one other neat little feature that the computerized testing format offers . . .

Instant feedback.

Yup—you read that right. As soon as you answer the last question, the computer offers you the choice either to view your "unofficial" score or to cancel your score. If you cancel your score, it is gone forever. There is no changing your mind, and you'll never know what your score actually was. The administration of the test *will*, however, be listed on your official Graduate Management Admission Council report to business schools; this is to prevent you from taking the test and canceling it six times and then scoring it the seventh time. Although schools do not generally frown on a single canceled score, a pattern of cancelations will tip off the admissions office to this strategy.

Nice try, though.

As with all other standardized tests, *resist* the knee-jerk urge to cancel your score. If you've trained for the exam, you'll know right away whether you've hit your mark or not. If something went wrong, and you know for certain or at least have a strong suspicion that you got a lot of the early questions incorrect, then you may want to cancel your score. Don't forget to factor the experimental questions into your equation. Remember that these questions have not been "road-tested" for difficulty and, as such, can be anomalous.

"If the questions seem really hard, remember that it is probably because you answered all of the previous questions correctly. I remember getting one question that was so complicated, it literally made my head hurt. It made me feel good, though, because I knew that it meant I had gotten all of the questions right up until then," Kanna recalls.

Dave agrees: "The start of every section really determines what your score will be. Start by camping on the first five to seven questions of each section. Be sure to get these correct. You will know your previous answer was good if the next question gets harder. If you can get through the first five to seven questions in every section perfectly, you'll be okay."

If you do not cancel your score, you will immediately receive an "unofficial score" of your verbal and math sections. The score is "unofficial" to protect ETS against any anomalies or glitches in the program, but it is almost always identical to the final score you receive in the mail about two weeks later. The Analytical Writing Assessment is not scored immediately, but your score on the writing component is sent with your "official" score report which should arrive approximately two weeks after you take the test.

How the Test Is Scored

The GMAT's math and verbal sections are independently given a 0–60 raw score and then combined into a total raw score and scaled to a final score ranging between 200 and 800. The analytical writing section is separately scored in half-point increments on a 0–6 scale, with a 6 being the highest score. The average GMAT score in recent years has hovered in the low 500s, and the average analytical writing score is around 4. Of course, the more competitive schools have much higher average scores. Both *U.S. News and World Report* and *Business Week* compile and publish data annually on the average GMAT scores at all accredited business schools, as well as GMAT score ranges, average undergraduate GPAs, number of applications received, percentage of applications accepted, and a host of other interesting data. Consult these sources to confirm the scores you'll need to be competitive at the schools of your choice.

At the time you receive your "unoffical" score in the testing center, you are given the option to forward the "official copy" of your scores to the schools you intend to apply to. The first five reports are sent free of charge. Additional reports can be sent for $25 each. When you go into the administration of the GMAT, be prepared with a list of the schools to which you would like to have your score reports sent.

What Is a "Good" GMAT Score?

According to *U.S. News and World Report*'s 2002 rankings, the nation's top ten business schools have an average GMAT score of 698, while the top twenty schools have an average of 687. But before you go reaching for a copy of *Law School Confidential* thinking that you'll never get into a top business program with your 620, stop. Remember that these numbers represent floating averages. Top business schools could fill their entire incoming classes with students boasting perfect GMAT scores, but they don't.

The rest of your background matters, too.

The GMAT is important, but it is only one factor in your application. Strong work experience, a good undergraduate GPA, and solid recommendations can help to overcome a somewhat subpar GMAT score.

Test Preparation

Because of the novelty this new testing format will present to most test-takers, and the importance of understanding the test architecture and how the computer selects questions of differing value based on prior responses, it is imperative that you study and train for both the content and the format of the GMAT. Every one of the mentors in this book began studying for the GMAT several months in advance of their test date, and six of the ten actually took a GMAT preparation course. Entire books have been written on the subject of how to master the GMAT, so we won't be reinventing that wheel here. Suffice it to say that you'll need to begin preparing for the exam several months before your anticipated test date.

"Four months prior to taking the GMAT, in June 1998, I mapped out a nightly study plan based on the ETS's *Official Guide to GMAT Review*. I spent maybe an hour a night answering questions from previous GMATs and tracked my progress over time. About one month prior to the big day, I took a "dry-run" practice exam at the Sylvan Learning Center, where I was going to take the real exam. This was *invaluable*, as I was able to familiarize myself with the testing environment, and gain confidence with the computer-based testing format," Brett recalls.

> "Take as many practice tests as possible. For me, this was the most effective approach. Doing this allowed me to understand and become familiar with both the types of questions asked, and the thought process and right approach to getting the answer. If I missed a question, I would spend a lot of time figuring out the correct answer and where I went wrong. I found this to be very helpful."
>
> —Andy

Start your preparation by purchasing the Educational Testing Service's *Official Guide to GMAT Review*. This guide contains actual past GMAT exams to give you a flavor of what a real exam actually entails. The downside is that the book contains only a few exams, and the exams that are in it are several years old and may not reflect recent trends on the test. Nevertheless, take a few sample tests and see how you do. If your scores are radically lower than the scores you'll need for admission to the schools of your choice, then you'll need to call in the reinforcements.

It should come as no surprise that your old friends at the Princeton Review and Stanley Kaplan offer GMAT preparation courses. Although these courses are pricey—now around $1,200—employees of these organizations routinely take the GMAT to track trends and changes on the exam, and have developed exemplars of each "type" of question posed by the exam, and strategies for conquering them, so there will be no mysteries come exam day. The price of admission includes the class, diagnostic exams, software, and unlimited drilling on specific types of questions, or entire exams, either online or in the organizations' many test centers around the country. Most people who take these courses improve their scores appreciably and consider them to be well worth the expense. "Taking the course is helpful both for the strategies they'll teach you, and for the discipline it forces on you," Kanna suggests.

When you are ready to actually take the test, you'll need to make an appointment to do so at one of more than four hundred licensed and authorized testing centers around the country and around the world. To find the authorized testing center nearest you, and/or to register for an appointment to take the computerized GMAT, go to www.ets.org/findctr.html and follow the GMAT link, or call 1-800-GMAT-NOW (1-800-462-8669). Each administration of the test costs $190 in the United States. Although the test is offered at certified test centers in a variety of foreign cities, costs are generally higher.

4

Applying to Business School

"The longest part of the journey is said to be
the passing of the gate."

— VARRO

THE NUTS AND BOLTS OF THE
APPLICATION PROCESS AND ANSWERS TO
THOSE NAGGING QUESTIONS

WHEN YOU APPLIED TO COLLEGE, your guidance counselor probably advised you to pick two or three schools in each of three tiers. The highest tier contained your "reach" schools, where your chances of admission were unlikely or uncertain, but most desired. The middle tier contained the schools which were a good numerical match for you, based on their mean GPA and SAT numbers, and where your chances of admission were good. Finally, the third tier contained your "safety" schools—one or two places, typically your state university system, where your chances of admission were virtually assured. For others among us, a single application to one's state university may, for financial or other reasons, have been the only choice.

The business school admissions process is an entirely different animal. The admissions criteria are different, the required documentation is different, there isn't always a state school available to you, and admission is virtually never assured. Accordingly, as you begin to consider applying to business school, the next two chapters are required reading. In this chapter, we discuss the "nuts and bolts" of the application process, and provide advice on how best to prevail in the increasingly competitive world of business school admissions. In the next chapter, we'll discuss these same nuts and bolts, and everything you ever wanted to know about the business school admissions process, with someone who is in an optimum position to counsel you about the process and how to succeed in it—Kristine Laca—Director of Admissions at the top-rated Tuck School of Business at Dartmouth College.

Onward, then!

GENERAL COMPONENTS OF A BUSINESS SCHOOL APPLICATION

The Personal Essay

As you review the various applications, you will find that some schools pose only three essay questions while others will ask six or seven. Do not be fooled. These essay questions, which often change from year to year and are often written by members of the admissions committees for very specific reasons, are extremely important to the fate of your application. Essay questions can cover a variety of topics. Some of the more common topics are highlighted below.

- How and why will an M.B.A. from this institution advance your career?
- Discuss a situation in which you exhibited leadership.

- Discuss a situation in which you experienced failure and what you learned from that experience.
- Discuss a situation in which you were faced with a serious ethical question and how you resolved it.
- Discuss your most significant life event to date, and why it was so.
- Discuss your ideal workday and what would make it so.
- Read and analyze the following case scenario and explain how you would resolve the problem . . .

The first thing to remember about responding to an essay question is to carefully read the question that is being asked, and answer that question clearly and directly. Do not try to force a story you want to tell into an application as an unresponsive answer to an essay question, and do not try to force an essay you wrote for another school into double-duty if it is not directly responsive to the question being asked. Business school admissions committees can smell these tactics from a mile away, and any sign of such laziness can be extremely detrimental to your application.

> "I simply wrote about me, what I hoped to become, and why I thought an M.B.A. would help me. The trick is to open up. The essays are often your first chance and, if you don't get an interview, your only chance to show the people in the admissions office who you are and why you would be a valuable addition to their program. Make the essays count!"
> —Dave

If you have the opportunity to craft responses to more open-ended questions, focus your responses on personal attributes or experiences that will help bring the picture of who you are as a person into sharper focus. Help to get the admissions reader behind the numbers in your application by bringing an interesting aspect of your background, travel, or work experience to life. Admissions committees typically use essays as a way of figuring out who you are, and what your personal goals and priorities are. Be sure that your essay responses serve you in this regard.

"Your essay topics should shed light on who you are, both as a businessperson and as a human being. Choose your topics strategically to help the person reviewing your file learn your story. Each of your essays should focus on one of the major areas of your life so that, when they are pieced together, the reviewer will understand the most critical aspects of who you are. Some things to consider discussing are why you chose your college, your college major, and your jobs after college, why you have made the career choices you have, what you hope to do professionally post-M.B.A., how an M.B.A. will help you to achieve those goals, and why the particular school to which you are applying is right for you."

—Toby

Anne agrees: "The main strategy I had with my essays was to think about them as a group, and use them to tell a consistent story throughout my application."

Coming up with thoughtful and responsive answers to essay questions is almost always the more difficult and time-consuming part of the process, so *take your time!* Do not set out to complete a response in an evening of work. Make a list of the essay topics you'll be faced with on your various applications, and look at them daily. Give your subconscious mind the opportunity to work with the topics, and give yourself the time to think about good responses for each one. Given the importance that admissions committees attribute to your essay responses, this is no time for a rush job.

Be sure to follow directions! If the essay imposes a page or word limit, stick to it. It is there for a reason, no matter how compelling your story. If the directions instruct you to use a certain font size or typeface, or to double-space your responses—for heaven's sake, follow the directions! You'd be amazed at how many people ignore simple instructions like these—and, as you'll see in the next chapter, these oversights are not lost on the admissions committees!

Once you've crafted what you think is a good response to an essay, walk away from it for several days, and then return to read it fresh. Check it for responsiveness and for compliance with the stated requirements. Give it a strong edit of your own, and then find a couple of trusted people to take a look at it. The best prospects for this job are people who are already in business school, since these people (1) just went through what you are going through; (2) will likely be more eager to help you, as a result; and (3) also probably have a pretty good idea what a good business school essay looks like.

"According to my friends who worked in the admissions office and read thousands of essays, a good essay met three primary criteria: (1) it was well written, succinct, and easy to follow; (2) it had a single theme and did not try to cram too much information in; and (3) is personal and unique to you," Matt advises. "Oh, and they also said essays mean *a lot* in the admissions process. Not putting in the time on your essays means you're not going to get in."

Recommendations

Generally, business schools will require at least one recommendation from a current or former business colleague. Again, be sure to follow the directions attached to the application. If the school asks for two applications, send them two. Not three. Not one. *Two.* If they ask for two recommendations from people in the business world who can comment on your abilities, don't send in a recommendation from one of your college professors. Follow directions!

This brings up the age-old question: Is it better to get a recommendation from the CEO of the Fortune 500 company you worked for who barely knew who you were, or from the obscure middle-level manager with whom you worked directly and closely for several years? Contrary to what you might think, this is a no-brainer. So who should it be? How many for the obscure middle-level manager? How many say the CEO?

If you picked the CEO . . .

You're wrong!

Your recommenders should be individuals with whom you worked directly, who know you, your work ethic, and your abilities well, and whom you believe can and will write you a thoughtful, detailed, and glowing recommendation.

> "A good recommender can attest to your character and has witnessed you under fire on several occasions. Your recommender does not need to be Shakespeare on a keyboard, but he does need to be able to recall the specific details of a given situation you faced and how you handled it, and to be able to sell that, and you, to the committee."
>
> —Dave

If you're not sure if your manager will give you a positive review, put the question to her directly and gauge her reaction to the question. If you sense enthusiasm, you have found your recommender. If you sense ambivalence, best you look elsewhere.

> "I had three recommendations: one from the managing director of my firm, who was also my direct supervisor; a second from a former client; and a third from my mentor of several years who had been my direct supervisor. A good recommender is someone who will speak very highly of you, who can give specifics to back up their claim, and who writes well."
>
> —Amy

Once you have lined up enough recommenders, do everything you can to make their job as easy as possible. Get the recommendation forms to them in a timely and organized fashion with pre-addressed and -stamped envelopes, and clearly stated due dates. Provide your recommenders with your résumé and a one-page autobiographical narrative of your background and experience. If they'll agree to it, sit down for a few minutes to discuss your various applications, and what it is that you're trying to get across to the particular schools to which you are applying.

Remember that the purpose of a recommendation is to give business schools an honest and sincere assessment of your work ethic and experience from someone who knows you well enough to comment thereon. Submitting some powerful "friend of a friend's" regurgitation of an outline of your key attributes that was written by his executive assistant will hurt, rather than help, your application.

"Rather than looking for someone senior to write your recommendation, go with someone who has worked with you on a day-to-day basis," Anne counsels. Kanna agrees: "Take the person with the less impressive title who knows you better."

Transcripts from All Academic Institutions Attended

You are going to need an official copy of your undergraduate transcript to be sent *directly* from your undergraduate university to the graduate programs to which you're applying. Take note: An *official* transcript is sent directly from the school to the graduate program; or has been enclosed in an envelope with a wax seal from the registrar's office returned to you, to be forwarded with your other application materials. It is *not* a photocopy of the transcript that you got when you graduated. You should expect to be charged a nominal fee of a few dollars for each official transcript you order, and you should expect that it might take up to three weeks for your undergraduate university to process your request and get your transcripts sent out. Be sure to give the university bureaucracy enough lead time.

GMAT and TOEFL Scores (If Applicable)

Test scores, too, in most cases, must be sent to your schools directly from the Educational Testing Service. During the test, you'll be given the opportunity to select five schools to which your scores will be sent free of charge. Take advantage of this, and arrive at the testing facility with a list in hand. If you do not have a list of schools prepared at the testing center, select the schools to which you think it is most likely that you will apply. If you have taken the GMAT more than once, your latest test scores plus the scores from your two most recent test administrations will be forwarded to schools.

Most U.S. business schools require that international applicants be able to fluently speak, read, write, and comprehend English. Therefore, applicants from non–English-speaking countries must take the TOEFL. Most schools require that TOEFL scores be no more than two years old. In many cases, applicants that have a Ph.D. from an English-speaking university are exempt from taking the TOEFL. Check with the schools to which you intend to apply for their most updated requirements.

Current Résumé

You will also have to provide a current résumé. Currently, business schools prefer to see a minimum of two years of post-collegiate work experience in their candidates, and most successful business school applicants have been working in the business world for three to five years after college. There are at least two compelling reasons for this. First, much of what business school teaches builds on general business skills and knowledge with which the professors will assume you are conversant. If you have no business experience, you will lack the foundational knowledge that animates many of these concepts. Second, much of the educational value at business school comes from the co-operative group work you will do with your classmates. If you or your classmates haven't had meaningful work experience before entering business school, you won't have much experiential knowledge to contribute to the cause, or to benefit from.

There are several items you will want to be sure to highlight in your résumé. Be sure to note your undergraduate university, year of graduation, major, your undergraduate GPA if it benefits you, your major, and any honors you received. Show your progression within the firm(s) you've worked for since graduation, including any leadership roles you've assumed. Discuss your community service participation, and any unique extracurricular activities with which you are or have been involved.

Leadership is an especially valued quality in a business school applicant. If you have served in any formal leadership roles, such as editor of your college newspaper, captain of an athletic team, or the organizer of a community outreach program, you should definitely note this experience on your résumé. Business schools are looking for self-starters who thrive when challenged and enjoy taking risks. These characteristics are consistent with individuals who will succeed as leaders in the business world and in their respective communities. If you feel you possess leadership qualities but do not have a specific role or position you can reference on your résumé, try to find a meaningful way to highlight these qualities in your essays or your interview.

A history of community service is another significant attribute that business schools look for, and one that is frequently overlooked by applicants. Community service gives schools a good indication of the character of an applicant, and the applicant's ability to work with others. Additionally, schools are looking for future alumni who will give back to the community once they've become successful. Some schools even grant scholarships to students who have devoted much of their time, if not their careers, to helping others. Even if your community service includes only occasional participation with your church's shelter or acting as a youth soccer coach, you should include it on your résumé.

If you have experienced quick promotions within your firm or career, be sure to highlight that fact clearly on your résumé. Show the progression, not simply the title you held most recently. This will help demonstrate to admissions-committee readers that you are diligent, hardworking, and someone who was thought worthy of promotion.

Lastly, you should point out any unique extracurricular activities in which you are or have been involved. This would include pursuits such as community service, but also discussion of significant hobbies, or the fact that you've recently hiked the entire Appalachian Trail. Be sure that the items you include as extracurricular activities say something about you, and that if you include them on your résumé, you are competent to speak about them in an interview.

The résumé you prepare for business schools should not be the same as the one you used for your most recent job application. Target your audience, update your accomplishments, remove any extraneous information or inapplicable purpose statements, and review all content for applicability. If you still have the fact that you ran the most successful paper route in town on your résumé, it's probably time to free up that space for something new.

Interviews

Some schools require interviews, others offer them without making them mandatory, while others do not even offer applicants the opportunity to interview. Depending on your personal style and interviewing ability, you may either yearn for the opportunity to make your case in an interview, or fear the very thought of it. Like it or not, if it is offered, the interview can be a tremendous opportunity to help strengthen your application. Further, electing to have a voluntary interview demonstrates your commitment to the school while failing to interview may be interpreted to the contrary.

There is simply no reason why you should ever fail to sign up for an interview at a business school that offers them. Period. If you're a horrible interviewer, then practice and get better. If you're afraid, then practice with other people to overcome your fear. You'll be required to interview for jobs soon anyway, so you might as well get used to it. Don't blow this incredible opportunity to animate your application materials, to put a face with your name in the mind of your interviewer, and to personalize the decision for those who will pass judgment on your candidacy at a particular school.

"Although some schools tell you that interviews are recommended but not required, don't be deceived. The interview gives you a singular opportunity to add additional depth to your application and to 'connect the dots' for your interviewer," Toby notes. "Unless you are a terrible interviewee and believe that your grades, work experience, and essays will speak for themselves, the interview can be extremely helpful."

When you schedule your interview, some schools give you the choice of an interview with a member of the admissions committee, a second-year student, or with an alumnus of the school. We strongly advise you to interview on campus and, if you have the option, to choose to interview with a member of the admissions committee whenever possible.

"I was living across the country, so I just called the admissions office when I was in town, long before interviews were being scheduled, and they were happy to talk to me then," Alden recalls.

Although admissions officers will tell you that an interview with a second-year student or an alumnus is "weighted the same" as an interview with a member of the admissions committee, there are at least a couple of visceral reasons why interviewing with a member of the admissions committee is preferable. First, members of the admissions committee actually *go* into committee and make decisions on files. In close calls in committee (and trust us, there are *many*), having the person who interviewed you in committee pulling for you can make the difference.

This presupposes, of course, that you favorably impress the interviewer during your interview! Members of the admissions committee work together all year, and have come to trust each other's judgment. At least on a psychological level, when the chips are down, they'll go with each other's recommendations before they go with a second-year student's or distant alumnus's interview recommendation. Furthermore, if you interview with a member of the admissions committee, you will get a phone number and contact person within the admissions office that you may use later if you have questions about your application's status.

All of this is *not* to say that you should be discouraged if your interviewer turns out to be a second-year student. Student interviewers typically work very hard to become members of the admissions committee (at most schools, it is quite competitive) and their scoring on interview score sheets *is* given equal weight with the interview scores turned in by members of the committee. The difference is in the psychology. If you have *the choice*, you'd rather have a booster in committee when the votes are cast, and at most schools, second-year students do not take files to committee.

Alumni interviews are typically offered to students who cannot make it to campus. Most foreign students, for example, are interviewed by alumni interviewers in foreign cities. Like second-year students, alumni interviewers are trained in the art of interviewing and how to score results. Their scores, like second-year students' scores, carry the same weight as the score given by a member of the admissions committee.

No matter who you interview with, however, do not make the mistake of arriving unprepared. Interviewing students consumes an inordinate amount of time and resources, so it should be clear that the schools that do interview place a *significant* emphasis on the interview component of the application.

So how do you prepare?

First, review the guidelines provided by each of the business schools with which you will be interviewing. Most schools give you at least some idea of what the focus of the interview will be. Know your résumé cold, and be prepared to discuss and defend anything on it. If you say you're fluent in Spanish, for example, you'd better be ready to do part of the interview in Spanish. Interviewers will probe for overstatements and other dishonest résumé representations in the interview, and any such shenanigans can be fatal to an application.

Be prepared to discuss your response to one or more of the school's essay questions. If you haven't reviewed the questions or your responses for some weeks, familiarize yourself with them the night before the interview, as, for many schools, the interview and the essay are the key components to your candidacy. You should also have a couple of good substantive questions about the school to ask the interviewer—things that are not answered by the application materials or other promotional materials.

There are several other common interview questions that were encountered by a majority of the mentors, including:

- Please walk me through your résumé.
- Why have you decided to apply to business school?
- Why are you applying to this business school?
- What do you offer that other candidates lack?
- What do you feel that you would contribute to this school?
- What do you enjoy doing when you're not working?
- Where do you see yourself professionally in ten years?

- What would your colleagues say is your biggest asset?
- What would your colleagues say is your biggest liability?
- Can I answer any questions about our program for you?

There are also several "rules of the road" for business school interviews that are best followed. First, you should treat the interview the same way you would treat a job interview. Dress the way you would for a formal business meeting unless you are specifically instructed by the admissions office to do otherwise. There is nothing more embarrassing than showing up in jeans and a sweater when everyone else is wearing a suit.

Second, do whatever it takes to arrive *early*. Interviews are typically on thirty-minute cycles, and because there is likely a whole slate of candidates following you, admissions officers tend to adhere strictly to their time limits. This is your thirty minutes to make your case to the committee. Losing half of it circling the block looking for a parking space communicates volumes to the admissions office.

Third, a quick, handwritten thank-you note after the interview is still expected. If you can use the note to trigger a memory of your interview in the admissions officer's mind, to keep your face fresh in his or her mind, so much the better.

Fourth—and this is a biggie, especially if you are interviewing with a second-year student—*don't* get too chummy with your interviewer. Even if you are older than the interviewer and even if you sense a camaraderie—keep the interview relatively formal and professional. No matter how comfortable the interview feels, the interview, including the downtime after it, is *never* a time to get too friendly. One interviewer we spoke with recalled a time when he had just concluded an interview with a strong candidate whom he was prepared to recommend to the committee. As the interview was concluding, the interviewee got up, extended a hand, and then asked, "So, are there a lot of hot single women around here?" That single (but significant) lapse in judgment caused a complete turnaround in the interviewer's impression of the candidate.

Don't let that happen to you.

Finally, resist the urge to bring your parents along to the interview. This is not your college tour all over again. Business schools are looking for independent, young leaders—not people who are still wedded to their parents for support. If your parents insist on making the trip with you, encourage them to walk around campus while you interview.

How Many Schools Should I Apply To?

Unlike with colleges and some graduate programs (notably, law schools), where programs of study are similar, business school programs have significant points of distinction. Some teach by what is called the "case method," while others use the "lecture method" (we discuss this distinction in a later chapter). Some schools are finance-oriented, while others emphasize marketing, operations, or nonprofit management. As such, the number of schools you apply to should be driven by how well the various programs meet your needs. Given the intense competition for seats in business school classes, once you have identified the schools that meet your interests, you should apply to as many of them as you can afford without compromising the quality of your applications.

"I did a lot of research up front, including visiting and reading websites, reading reviews, talking to alumni, talking to current students, and discussing the various choices with people I respected," Matt recalls. "As a result, I applied to the three schools that met my requirements—the schools that were smaller, very teamwork-focused, and had sound reputations in the fields in which I was interested."

Kanna had a different experience:

"I applied to Harvard, Stanford, and Kellogg. I applied to Harvard because I went to undergrad there, and to Stanford and Kellogg because I liked their focus on the culture of the experience in addition to the academics. I went to Kellogg because it is the only place I got in, but I should have known more about these schools before I applied. I would not have been happy with Harvard's more competitive, case-driven approach. Kellogg's team focus was much more appropriate for my work style. I got lucky, but I should have known about that before applying."

If you are dead set on going to business school *next year*, try to include a range of schools in your application list. Of course, there is no way you can know which schools you will and will not gain admission to, but, based on a school's average GMAT and undergraduate GPA ranges, you should be able to discern probabilities for most of the schools on your list. As it did when you applied to college, your list should include a couple of "reach" schools, a couple of "probables," and at least one or two schools you feel relatively certain you will earn admission to.

If you have some flexibility in your plans, you can afford to apply only to the top programs, or the programs that best suit your needs. "I applied to only one school," Alden explains, "because after looking at the profiles of the top twenty schools, I decided that Yale was the only school that could provide the kind of nonprofit-management education that I sought. If there is a clear choice, you are better off concentrating on and making your case to the school you really want to attend."

If you are unsuccessful in your first attempts at admission, many of these schools will offer you feedback on your application—including specific advice about how to make your application stronger. Many business schools look favorably upon reapplicants, especially those that have heeded the advice of the admissions committee and met the concerns raised in a prior year.

In case you were wondering, the mean and median number of schools the mentors applied to was four; the high was six; and the low was Alden's single (and successful) application to the Yale School of Organizational Management's nonprofit-management program.

WHEN SHOULD I APPLY?

Business schools have different numbers of application rounds, and treat these rounds differently. For instance, some may offer an early-action round where you can be assured of a decision before the winter holidays. Some have the policy of rolling applicants waitlisted in an early round into the next round; while other schools address all waitlisted individuals after all rounds have been completed. Still others use a true "rolling admissions" policy where individual decisions are made as individual applications come in. These schools can inform you of your acceptance, waitlist status, or rejection at any point in time.

Although many admissions officers will tell you that your chances of admission are roughly the same in any round, our research suggests otherwise.

"Submit your application as early as possible," Dave counsels. "I have heard from several people that their schools came back to them and said, 'All is well, but we want you to improve your GMAT score before we can accept you.' The earlier you apply, the more time you'll have to respond to such requests."

Brett agrees: "Don't procrastinate! Admissions offices do *not* spread out acceptance letters evenly across rounds, and as such, a school may fill 75 percent of its available seats by the midpoint of the application season, making your chances for admission significantly lower if you apply late in the game."

We encourage you to apply to business schools as early in the application process as you possibly can. There are several reasons for this line of thinking.

First, applying early in the process, particularly in a nonbinding early-action round, exhibits your enthusiasm for a particular school—a fact which does make a difference. Admissions committees know you will likely be applying to several programs and view early-round applications as coming from the students who are most eager about their school. If you're waitlisted, this may help to distinguish you from second- and third-round applicants.

Second, in the early rounds (and particularly in the first round), admissions committees won't necessarily have a complete picture about how selective they need to be with applicants since these applications are the first it has seen for the year. Committees do tend to target well-qualified candidates early in the process, and as such, if you are a well-qualified candidate in an early round, you may be more likely to get a favorable decision, since early-round applications have the benefit of being considered when the fewest number of spaces in the class have been filled.

Finally, in schools that roll waitlisted applicants forward into subsequent rounds, if you are waitlisted in an early round, you may get as many as three additional "looks" from the admissions committee. If you apply in the final round, you get only one look, and will compete for the few remaining seats in the class not only with the people in your admissions round, but with all of the well-qualified waitlist candidates from all of the previous rounds.

"Applying in the early-to-middle part of the process can boost your chances of success," Toby explains. "If a school is unsure about your candidacy, they can pass you to the next round of reviews, thus effectively giving you additional chances as you go through the process."

If your application is complete, your GMAT score represents your best effort, and there is nothing significant you feel that you could do to better your application materials, get them in as early as you can.

5

On What Really Matters in the
Business School Application:
A Candid Look at the Application Process
with Kristine Laca, Director of Admissions
of the Tuck School of Business at Dartmouth

"Knowledge is of two kinds . . . knowing a subject ourselves or knowing
where we can find information upon it."
— SAMUEL JOHNSON

*Kristine, first of all, I'd like to thank you for taking the time out of your
busy travel schedule to meet with us and to speak directly to the future
generations of business school students who will read this book. As you
know, the focus of this book is to provide those business school students
with advice about how to get the most out of the process. There is
nothing more vexing to prospective business school students than the
somewhat unpredictable nature of the business school admissions process, so I'm really thrilled that you agreed to participate in this project.*

I'm happy to be a part of your latest book and to be as helpful
as I can be in providing advice and suggestions to your readers.

*Let's start at the beginning. What compelled you to switch from a po-
sition in strategic planning and marketing for Nike to something as
radically different as chairing the admissions department at a business
school?*

It had to do with a change in priorities, and a lot of that had to do with having a child. My husband and I were blessed by the birth of our daughter, but at that time, I was working internationally for Nike. It just wasn't tenable for me to have to travel to Amsterdam or to Hong Kong for a week and a half at a clip. Therefore, I began to think about doing something different—something where my energies and passions could be directed more towards helping people. I knew of Tuck's tremendous reputation from when I was in business school. When I heard about the position, it sounded intriguing. There is a significant component of marketing and strategic planning in admissions, which is my background. This role is a nice opportunity to contribute and learn at the same time.

Do the directors and deans of admissions from the various business schools talk with each other, or do you live in an insular world where you find yourself trying to lure students away from "the competition"?

We actually do talk. In fact, I was just on the phone with my counterpart at Harvard trying to ascertain how applications are trending this year. It is refreshing that, within this industry, we can share a lot of information. I don't think students realize that the admissions directors of the various schools are more collaborative than competitive.

When you say you share information, what kind of information do you mean?

Let me assure people that we do not share information about specific applicants—nothing proprietary or confidential, but we do share trends. We discuss the bigger picture topics that can help us determine whether the results we are seeing are outliers, or consistent with what is happening across the top schools.

Does it get competitive between schools?

It's not competitive and far from insular, which is so refreshing. We all work with great institutions and there are strong points of differentiation amongst the schools. Everyone is very confident and proud of his or her program, so you don't get into the sense of competitiveness that you might find elsewhere. I am always pleasantly surprised at how helpful everybody is, especially at a time when things are changing. Last year, for example, our applications were up forty percent!

Was that consistent with overall trends in business school, or was Tuck higher than most?

Tuck's application increase was a bit higher than most; the average across the industry was between 10 and 20 percent.

Do you attribute that to the collapse of the dot com boom?

That played a role, but more people were interested in applying to Tuck because of our program and lifestyle issues. Living in Hanover is not the same as living in a big city; there is a tremendous sense of community here. After September 11, many people reevaluated their priorities and placed a greater emphasis on community and the "experience" of business school. Studying at Tuck has always been more than just earning a degree. On top of that, the strong ranking in the *Wall Street Journal* put Tuck on more people's radar screens and helped more prospective students appreciate that there can be different models for business schools.

Let's get into the process itself. Who is on the admissions committee at Tuck?

It is a large team of people. Within admissions, we have a group that focuses on marketing, events, and connecting with prospective students. We have a second team that is responsible for operations and systems. With over three thousand applications, there is a lot to process. This year, we've moved to online applications, thus creating more behind the scenes work. The final group is responsible for both the recruiting and enrollment of students.

That is the team that comprises the admissions committee itself. We are also supported by a dedicated group of second year student interviewers and alumni interviewers.

Okay, let's focus on the admissions committee itself—the core group that decides who gets in and who doesn't. Who comprises that committee?

There are voting members of the committee and a few non-voting members who help track applications and decisions. The voting members are the assistant and associate directors and myself. We want to keep the committee team small so that we can level-set and achieve both familiarity and consistency with one another.

What are the backgrounds of the people on the admissions committee?

Some of us have M.B.A.s—everyone has an advanced degree. Some have recruiting backgrounds or were leaders in Tuck's Career Services office. Others have spent significant time on the business side—both domestically and internationally. The committee is an accomplished, multicultural, and multiracial team with a clear perspective on what makes a student successful at Tuck.

Can you give me a general overview of the process?

We give prospective students the option to download the application, but almost everyone files the application electronically. As we receive applications, letters of recommendation and interviewer feedback, all of the materials are collated into one file. Once an application is complete, the assistant director in charge of the overall process assigns the file to a reader.

Could you explain the process of admissions "rounds"?

There are four separate times that we consider applications for admission. The first is our Early Action round, with a deadline in mid-October. We then have three additional rounds: one with a deadline in November, one in January, and the final one in April.

How does the Early Action process work?

When applicants know that Tuck is their first choice, Early Action allows them to learn as quickly as possible whether they are accepted. About 25 percent of the candidates we saw in our Early Action round were re-applicants, including many who were waitlisted last year and have, in some cases, turned down offers at other schools, worked for another year, and applied again. This round was a response to conversations I had with people on the waitlist who were phenomenal candidates and who would have been admitted without hesitation if we had a few more seats in the class. In trying to decide what was the best thing to do for those applicants, we decided to develop a nonbinding Early Action round for people who want to express a clear first choice.

If someone knows that a school is their first choice, would you advise him or her to apply early?

If you know you are interested in attending a specific school and your candidacy is as strong as it can be, you should apply as early as possible. Nevertheless, if prospective students feel that their application can be strengthened in some substantial way— for example, they struggled with the GMAT and know they could do better by taking the test again, but retaking the test means that they won't be able to apply Early Action—I would encourage those students to take the test again and apply later. The only advantage in the Early Action round is the notification timing. I feel strongly that Early Action should be a process where we provide a sense of closure for our applicants. Just make sure that you are putting your best foot forward if you decide to apply early.

Is the admissions standard more or less stringent for those who apply Early Action?

A person who is applying Early Action is not evaluated any differently than other candidates. The only caveat is that, as we start looking at the early applicant pool, we only have 240 available seats. If we see a large number of exceptional candidates in the early pool, we will admit those candidates—so gaining admission becomes more difficult as we move through the rounds in a numeric sense because there are fewer seats available. We do not allocate a certain number of seats to each round.

So the take-home message is to get your application in as early as possible?

Absolutely. Your chances are better at the beginning of the process when the largest number of seats are still available.

Who conducts your interviews?

Members of the admissions committee conduct interviews, so that means that I also conduct a fair number. We also have a very dedicated group of second-year student interviewers and 150 alumni interviewers around the world.

So if someone comes to campus for an interview, who is going to do the interview?

If you come to campus—and we strongly encourage everyone to come to campus—you will be interviewed either by one of the committee members or by a second-year student. It is a random process, but all interviews are weighted the same regardless of who interviews you.

Well, wait, though. I'd want to have my interview with one of the committee members. I'd want to establish that personal connection since that person is actually going to be in committee deciding my fate. Wouldn't I?

It honestly will not make a difference. To give you an example, I am currently reading all of the files that are not recommended for admission. In those piles, there are people I personally interviewed and really liked. Unfortunately, despite a good interview, there were other things about their application that concerned committee members. The interview is just a piece of the overall picture. The fact that the person interviewed well with me did not end up changing the outcome.

So how do the alumni interviewers play in?

When you visit our website, you can request an interview in Hanover or in any larger city around the world. Everyone who visits Hanover is offered the opportunity to interview. If you cannot come to campus, we try to arrange interviews with alumni interviewers, committee members or occasionally second-year student interviewers. The feedback that we get from the interviewers is extremely important to us.

What happens in an interview? What questions do you ask, and what is it that you are looking for?

We try to ask questions that we cannot answer through the application. I would rather not use an interview to rehash the resume or ask about test scores. We are trying to get a sense of who the person is. I want to know what motivates our applicants, what interests them, how much they value a sense of community. We want to attract and select those people who not only want a great education, but who are also interested in participating in and contributing to a strong community—and that is something that you don't necessarily pick up from a paper application. Our interviews are thirty minutes long. They are straightforward and are far from stressful.

What happens after the interview? Is there a form that the interview is evaluated on?

We have a standardized form. What we are looking for is no secret; it is published in all of our materials. Fundamentally, we are looking for people who can demonstrate merit in six areas.

The first is academic excellence. We want to accept applicants who will thrive in this academic environment. You cannot comprehensively evaluate that in an interview; most of that comes from the application. Second, we are looking for someone who is both a strong team player and a leader. We look for evidence of these attributes in work, the community, and in university. Third, we are looking for people who are able to set and attain goals as well as overcome challenges. Again, we are looking at accomplishments across a broad spectrum. Fourth, we look for strong interpersonal skills—people who can influence, inspire, and motivate. As a leader, you need to have excellent communication skills. Again, this is something that you cannot judge from paper alone. You have to sit down and talk to somebody to get a sense of how well he or she can connect with other people. I ask myself: How am I going to feel if this person is in my study group? Fifth, I am looking for diversity in a very broad sense. We are looking for a breadth of perspectives, experience, industry backgrounds, and different levels of involvement. As a student, we make a commitment to you that you will be able to learn as much outside the classroom as you are going to learn inside the classroom. The only way that we can assure this is to offer admission to the best people from a very diverse set of backgrounds. Finally, we are looking for students who want to make a difference in the community. This is something that you can very clearly see both from talking with people and from reading about activities. This is a community where an individual can make a tremendous difference. We have many traditions at Tuck that started because one person said, "we should do something about this" or, "we should do that differently."

Okay, so that brings us to the GMAT. People panic about it. Its computerized test format can be very foreign to people. How much does the GMAT score matter to you, and to your committee? How is it used?

The GMAT is one indicator. We encourage people to look at

both the mean and the range of GMAT scores. For example, our average is close to 700. That by itself may seem intimidating to some people . . . but our range is very broad—from 530 to 800. So, that should tell you that we value a number of things, not just the GMAT. We look at the GMAT to help answer the question, "Can this person do the work?" I do not want to put a student in a situation in which he or she is going to struggle. There are a lot of different things that go into answering and validating the assumption, "Yes, this person can do the work."

What, beside the GMAT score and transcript, helps you answer that question?

In our letters of recommendation, we solicit confidential feedback about a candidate's intellectual ability. We also try to get a sense of intellectual curiosity and ability from the answers to essay questions.

How do you evaluate undergraduate performance? You mentioned that performance, particularly in quantitative courses, is critical. How much do you pay attention to people's GPAs, especially for people who have been out of school for a while, and how do you compare, for example, a 3.5 from a top school with a 3.5 from a lesser known school?

The most important question is: Can this person do the work? A poor college performance may give rise to a whole separate set of questions about why the candidate was not successful in college. I will want to get a sense that the prospective student is both mature and understands the level of commitment needed to be successful in a program like Tuck. Sometimes you have to look to what else was going on in a person's life that might have made it more difficult for him or her to do well. We are always looking for those pieces. We do look at where you studied, but we never limit ourselves to people from certain schools. For example, you may have studied at a lesser-known school but graduated at the top of your class. We also look at what you studied.

So, it is sort of an individualized, person-by-person examination?

It is a very individualized review. We are always trying to make the best and most objective assessment across the entire pool.

What's your position on people who apply directly out of college?

Tuck looks for people who have work experience, but I would never discourage exceptional undergraduates from applying. Occasionally we see candidates who are outstanding and who have significant accomplishments other than work experience. While I might consider that person for admission, I might also offer a contingent admission for the following year so that he or she can gain additional experience and perspective.

I didn't know that conditional admission was an option.

It would depend on the individual circumstances. Most business schools are looking for people with three to five years of business experience. Think about it from the perspective of a business school study group. If you have four people with three to five years of consulting, finance, marketing, and nonprofit experience, and one student who is right out of college, is that fair to the others? In some cases, an additional year of experience could turn a strong candidate into an exceptional candidate. In other cases, direct admission might make sense.

So the take-home message here is that working after college for a period of years is what most applicants do, and that if you choose to apply directly to business school from college, you ought to have a pretty compelling reason in your experience or application materials to explain why you think you're ready to attend business school?

Yes.

Okay, let's move on to the essay questions. How do you use the essay questions and how important are they to an applicant's overall application?

Our essay question this year is a case. I wanted to have a question that would make people think about difficult business decisions where there are conflicting priorities or senses of value. The question has elements of both social and business issues and asks you to make some tough decisions. The question is: "You are a newly appointed general manager to a mining company in a third world country. There have been peaceful protests in the community asking for a share of the mining profits to build an infrastructure of clean water and electricity. Building the infrastructure would cost eight million dollars. The government, a military dictatorship, has been nonresponsive. Your company is paying twenty million dollars in taxes. Your business's after-tax profit is fifty million, which is the minimum level that will assure your team makes its bonus. Your team has worked very hard this year. What do you do?" What we are asking people to do with this question is to analyze the situation and to develop a plan of action. We are looking at people's ability to take a leadership position. The ingenuity and creativity that some people are showing in answering this question has been wonderful.

Is there a common mistake that you see on applications over and over again that people ought to know about?

I like to see people who are honest about both their strengths and shortcomings. None of us are perfect—we all have our areas to improve. That's part of being human.

Going to letters of recommendation, what are you looking for in those?

Find references who know you well enough to be able to answer the questions that we are asking. One big mistake that applicants make is that they ask for letters of recommendation from someone with a big title versus asking a person who really knows them and who can provide us with good insight. We often receive recommendations from presidents and CEOs of Fortune 500 corporations. When you read the comments, you realize that very few of the writers had direct interaction with the applicant.

What about sending more letters than are requested?

In rare instances, sending an extra letter of recommendation is helpful but only if the extra letter can help explain something that might otherwise be a concern in the application. Beyond those rare exceptions, two letters written by people who know an applicant well usually suffice.

What would be something that would be worth explaining in an extra letter of recommendation?

Short tenure in a job, inconsistent academic performance, job termination . . . There was one recent applicant who was involved in an incident in college where disciplinary action was taken. One of the letters of recommendation, an extra letter, was from the dean of student life who was involved in the incident. Hearing from the dean made me more comfortable with what had happened; this was an excellent use of an extra letter of recommendation. Nevertheless, those are very rare instances. We want to read the important information relevant to your candidacy; however, it is not wise to inundate the admissions committee with lots of unnecessary paper.

With respect to a candidate's employment history, is there anything in particular that you are looking for that would set someone ahead in your mind?

We look for people who are able to take on leadership roles and make a difference. I look for applicants who can set and achieve goals, who can overcome obstacles, and who can employ creative solutions. Part of effective business management is being able to think creatively about problems.

What is the importance of race, ethnicity, and cultural background in your admissions decisions?

On the whole, we strive to have a diverse class. It's in the school's best interest and student body's best interest to have a diverse class of highly qualified students. I define diversity in more ways than just race, ethnicity, or cultural background. It gets back to experience, perspectives, thoughts, future interests—all of those things contribute to the richness of the perspective that a person is going to bring to business school. There is a tremendous benefit to having that level of diversity.

And what effect do legacies have?

Legacy candidates, people who are direct relatives of alumni, are evaluated on their own merits and against the pool. There usually are a few students in every class who are legacies, but that says more about our alumni passion than preferential treatment. Tuckies are passionate about their school, and that passion is sometimes handed down from generation to generation. Given that we were the first graduate school of business management, we have second, third, and sometimes fourth-generation applicants, but the evaluation process is the same across the board. There are no special admission advantages in being a legacy.

Okay, so now let's get into the nuts and bolts of the decision-making process itself. Is there some sort of screening process that goes on at the beginning of each round to cull out the likely admits from the likely denies?

No. We review every application multiple times.

How does that process work?

It's an extensive review process. Three people will read a file before it goes into committee. Those reviews are done "blind," which means that the second person to read an application does not see the comments of the first reviewer. This allows us to have several impartial reviews for each application. Additionally, I read every application that is nominated for committee.

What about the rest of the files—what happens to those?

As a reader, you have three options: recommend to admit, to

deny, or to waitlist. We cull down the group between the second and third reader and again between the third reader and committee so that we have a reasonable number of files in committee. This allows us to focus on those top candidates and have an open, passionate debate about each one. When it is recommended that a candidate not be moved to the next reader or to committee, I am the final person who signs off on the decision. And yes, there are times when I over-ride the recommendation and ask that a file be read again or moved into committee.

What do you mean by "go to committee"?

In committee, we assign the specific folders to specific committee members. Those committee members are responsible for presenting those candidates to the rest of the committee. Once we get into committee, we are no longer talking about GMAT, GPA, leadership, or accomplishments. If you're in committee, you're there because we are convinced that: you can do the work, you have leadership potential, you understand teamwork, you have demonstrated significant accomplishments, you have strong work experience, and you are someone who can be a contributor to the Tuck community. So it essentially becomes: who are the best candidates in the pool?, and what will each of those candidates bring to the class?

What percentage of the overall applicant pool makes it to committee?

We do not have a set percentage. The number of applications that go to committee depends on the strength of the pool. If it is a great pool, more applications will be presented in committee. We simply extend the number of days of committee.

How do you decide who presents which files in committee?

It usually makes sense for a person who has some familiarity with the applicant to be the person presenting. Other times, we may ask a committee member to present all candidates from a specific country or industry. As an applicant is presented, there are always at least two other people in the room who have reviewed and commented on the file—including myself. If the applicant interviewed with one of the committee members, there might even be a fourth person.

So once you are in committee, how are decisions made?

We discuss the merits of each candidate in detail and from many perspectives. Any applicant who is reviewed in committee is a great candidate and could be a fantastic contributor to Tuck, so at this point, it becomes tough. As I mentioned, we are trying to build an outstanding, diverse, and multifaceted class, and that is why, as we are making the decisions, we have adjunct members keeping track so that we can see how the class is taking shape. For example, have we already admitted a large group of talented people from the same industry? Those are good pieces of information for the committee to know. Much of this is the art in putting the class together.

What happens to people on your waitlist?

I don't have a target number of people for the waitlist, but I like us to have a manageable number. We like to maintain close communication with all of the people on our waitlist, and you cannot do that if the number becomes too unwieldy. Some people will naturally remove themselves from the waitlist as they get into other strong programs, and we respect that. Let's say that you are put on the waitlist in the November round. When we hold our January round committee, we look at the January pool and the waitlist from November. We will take the strongest candidates from that combined pool.

What should someone on your waitlist do to reaffirm his or her interest and give himself or herself a little edge?

I think it is important for people on our waitlist to make sure that their desire to come to Tuck is known. You never know what is going to happen as you get very close to the first day of classes, and it is always critical for us to know who at the top of the waitlist might be willing to enroll with very little notice. We're very active in communicating with the people on our waitlist. We always try to give our waitlisted applicants an honest assessment of the situation.

How do the **U.S. News and World Report, Business Week, Wall Street Journal, Financial Times,** *and* **The Economist** *rankings of business schools play into your thinking? Does it affect how you do things in order to make your average GMAT score, GPA, admit rate, and yield numbers "come out right"?*

The reality is that the rankings don't affect the process. In addition to some very sound methodology, there is a lot of subjectivity in the rankings. I look at all rankings with a grain of salt.

Do you feel pressure from the marketing and P.R. side to make sure that your annual numbers move you in the right direction in the rankings?

Absolutely not. I have had several conversations with our dean, and he has been very supportive that we enroll the right people, irrespective of the numbers, rankings, or outside perceptions.

What advice do you have for students about how to best use the different ranking systems to help identify schools that are right for them?

I would look at the methodology and not just at the results. Each of the different surveys and rankings are measuring different things. The *Wall Street Journal,* for example, asks recruiters about their experience and satisfaction with the performance of graduates from different M.B.A. programs. Another ranking is measuring student satisfaction. I think each of these surveys, in isolation, has something interesting to say, but there is also inherent subjectivity. Do the research. Talk to alumni. Visit the school. Talk to current students. Attend classes. Each school is very different. What might be the perfect environment for one person is not for the next person. Someone who is purely motivated by the rankings may end up studying at the wrong school.

You did mention before, though, that someone's quantitative skills on the GMAT might be scrutinized a little bit more closely than their qualitative skills.

That's just the reality. We have a highly quantitative curriculum, and that's not going to change whether your career aspirations are in marketing or nonprofit management.

You're sitting with a friend, and you have a couple of minutes to tell her what she needs to know to succeed in the application process. What do you tell her?

I would recommend that she first take the time to understand what was important to her. Then, I would suggest that she do her research. I'd tell her to talk to current students and alumni. I would tell her to visit the schools that interested her most. As far as the application process goes, I'd tell her to be herself and to make sure to paint a clear picture of why she is interested in a specific program. If you focus on demonstrating who you are as a person and the qualifications that you have as a candidate, you can't really go wrong. Don't make this process more than it should be.

Now, what advice would you give to students who did not get in to their first-choice schools? Should they wait another year and reapply, or just go their third- or fourth-choice schools and move on with their lives?

I think it gets back to understanding what is important to you. You can find many schools that will successfully deliver in some fashion against the areas that are important to you. If you had your heart set on one school and it does not work out, try to get feedback from that school. Even if the school does not offer feedback, think about what you feel were the strengths and weaknesses of your application. Whenever I start a feedback session, I ask that very question of the applicant. Nine times out of ten, the applicant knows exactly what areas could be improved. Ultimately, an applicant with options must assess his or her personal tolerance for waiting a year. Historically, we look very favorably upon reapplicants who have been able to make their candidacies stronger in the specific areas that needed to be strengthened. So, try to address whatever is discussed in the feedback session and apply again.

Who gets this feedback?

Members of the admissions committee offer feedback to any applicant who would like to apply again. It is something that we do in the summer on a first-come, first-serve basis.

What are the types of things that you would give feedback on?

All sorts of things are discussed in a feedback session. We might suggest improving written expression. We might discuss our concern about a lack of involvement outside of work. Sometimes, we suggest that a candidate take a class or two to help provide them with additional quantitative coursework or stronger English skills. It all depends on where the candidate has the ability to improve.

Before we wrap up, is there anything else you want people to know?

Just that the admissions process is not a mysterious thing that happens in a back room. We have done our best to make the process as open as possible. Ultimately, we are trying to make the best decisions given the information that we have at our disposal. Do your best to show us who you are as a potential student at our school and have the foresight to help us answer any questions that might arise about your candidacy.

6

On Choosing a School

"The direction in which education starts a man
will determine his future life."

— PLATO

CHANCES ARE, YOU know the names and reputations of several of the "top" schools before you even begin to do any research about them. *Business Week, U.S. News and World Report,* and the *Wall Street Journal* all publish the ubiquitous and well-publicized lists of the top business schools every year, and these rankings often play a critical role in the competitiveness of the admissions process at a particular school.

"Rankings are a fact of life. Like it or not, a school's reputation plays an extremely important role in determining what recruiters will come to campus, and how wide the doors will be held open when you go looking for job opportunities through an independent job search," Toby admits. "As such, while rankings should not be a sole determinant for you, they should play a critical role in your decision-making process."

Alden agrees: "Evaluate the industry and environment in which you expect to work, and decide whether a school's rank and reputation are important to the people who will be hiring you, as reputation varies greatly by industry and geographic region. That said—in my opinion, if you are not going to go to one of the top schools, or one that specializes in a specific field that you are interested in, or one that is well thought-of in the industry and geographic region in which you expect to work, you are probably better off getting your business education on the job."

While a school's national ranking is certainly important, be sure you have thoroughly researched the schools themselves and developed a list of the meaningful criteria that you will use to differentiate the schools for yourself.

"The rankings are important in that they provide general information about a school's relative strengths," Brett notes. "Looking at the numbers in a vacuum, though, is meaningless. Applicants should view these rankings as one source of information. *U.S. News and World Report, Business Week,* and the *Wall Street Journal* provide plenty of useful information regarding acceptance rates, average starting salaries, and so forth, but no publication should serve as the *de facto* source of a conclusion about a school's relative merits."

A discussion of some of the more important criteria to consider follows below.

ACADEMIC FOCUS AND STRENGTHS

Aside from their overall national rankings available in the aforementioned publications, many schools have a reputation for excellence in a particular business discipline like marketing or finance. If you've followed our advice in the first three chapters of this book, you should already have a clear vision of *why* you are going to business school and what you hope to get out of it. As such, you should also have at least some idea about what areas of academic discipline are most important to you. Take the time to research the schools, and determine each school's strengths and weaknesses. The Internet has made this process much easier than it used to be. In the event that you can't get all the information from a school's website, call the admissions office or the placement office and ask your unanswered questions.

Once you have completed your research about schools and their areas of academic strength and weakness, put this information to good use. Don't just blindly follow the lists. Compare your long-term career goals to the strengths and weaknesses of each school on your list. You might be better off at a slightly lower-ranked school known for its excellence in the discipline of greatest interest to you (marketing, for example), than you would be at a higher-ranked school not particularly known for that discipline. Because business schools teach many different disciplines and prepare their students for many different positions in business, it is essential that you choose a school that offers a strong curriculum in the discipline in which you plan to build a career.

No idea what that is? Then you are not ready to apply to business school. Time to go back to chapter 1 and work through the questions there until you have a better idea of what your goals are. The two-year business school experience is too short to spend half of it fumbling around trying to find direction.

THE IMPACT OF REGIONALITY

Large corporations spend an extraordinary amount of time and money recruiting future employees at schools with nationally ranked programs. After years of hiring M.B.A. graduates, the top U.S. and international firms have narrowed the list of schools at which they carry out extensive on-campus recruiting—and, not coincidentally, that list is usually limited to the top fifteen schools, and the schools in the immediate vicinity of the companies' largest corporate offices. Companies schedule information sessions, interviewing timetables, and numerous social events at these schools throughout the school year, making the job search much easier. If your intentions are to use business school as a stepping-stone to a position at a large national or international corporation, you should work hard to get admitted to one of the top fifteen programs.

Programs with strong regional reputations, however, can play to your advantage if you know you are ultimately looking to secure a job within the sphere of that regional school's influence. Many companies, for example, like to hire graduates of local business school programs because there is an increased chance that someone who is applying to employment positions in the same city or region as the school, actually likes the area and wants to settle there. Firms are interested in retaining the employees they train, and knowing that a candidate likes the area eliminates one of the big challenges to retention. Many companies also simply like to support local universities by hiring graduates from these schools.

"Regional bias is an important factor related to job-hunting that you should consider," Toby advises. "You need to find out whether the school you are considering attracts recruiters from locations in which you are interested in working."

For applicants who already know they want to end up in a particular city post-graduation, regional bias is an especially important consideration. "For applicants with a specific geographic focus, it may make sense to consider local M.B.A. programs," Andy advises. "Oftentimes, these programs will have a much stronger local network of professionals to help in the job search and ongoing relationship-building."

"Students from 'lower-ranked' or lesser-known business schools can do very well in recruiting if they are aggressive in looking for employment," Anne notes. "It's still about the person, not just the school."

Almost all business schools track where their students find employment, and should be able to provide you with job placement information for their recent graduating classes. If you are even considering attending a regional or local business school, you owe it to yourself to study this information. Attending a school without a strong national reputation may hinder your chances of getting a job outside the school's state or geographic region. Don't matriculate at East Boise State University Business School if your goal is to get a corporate position with a firm in Miami.

SIZE

Entering class sizes at business schools range from under one hundred to nearly a thousand—and yes, in this instance, at least, size *does* matter. For starters, the size of a business school's entering class can directly affect your ability to gain admission to a seat in that class. Schools with lower class sizes tend to have lower acceptance rates, which can be a factor of the school's high standards, fewer seats to offer, or a combination of both. You may instinctively find yourself leaning toward smaller programs because they suggest a more intimate atmosphere. Though there are several advantages to the smaller programs, there are also some drawbacks.

Before you make your determination solely on the number of people in your entering class, be mindful of the fact that most schools divide their first-year students into "sections" to facilitate a more intimate experience. Don't automatically assume that the larger the school is, the larger the number of students in each classroom will be. The number of students in a class is, of course, ultimately determined by the number of professors teaching, and into how many sections the first-year class is divided. Determine the average of class sizes for the first-year core required classes, and the range and average of elective classes to get a better sense for what the experience at a particular school will be like. Again, if this information is not contained in a school's admissions brochure, on the school's website, or in other readily available materials, simply call the school's admissions office and ask!

Although larger schools tend to break down the sizes of their entering classes to accommodate smaller class sizes, there are still some general considerations to undertake when choosing between larger and smaller institutions.

Having fewer classmates overall is likely to make your business school experience more intimate and less intimidating. Facilities such as computer labs and study spaces may be less crowded than at other institutions. You will get to know more of your classmates well, and, as such, it may be easier to develop stronger friendships and business relationships that you can carry out into the world when you graduate. The alumni networks at smaller programs are often especially strong, providing you with a solid network of multigenerational business contacts after graduation, and also, especially strong tendencies of alumni to seek out and hire from their alma mater.

The larger programs, however, also come with their own raft of advantages, including a larger concentration of "big-name" professors, more significant recruiting and career development services, and improved intercultural educational opportunities, since larger programs tend to seat greater numbers of international students in each class. Thus, attending a larger program typically affords you increased opportunities to work with and learn from a greater variety of students.

Larger programs are generally also better funded than smaller programs, which is usually reflected in the facilities offered to students. These institutions are likely to have larger computer labs and study areas, more meeting rooms, and a better technologic infrastructure. Larger programs are also typically able to offer higher salaries, which helps in the attraction and retention of professors at the forefront of their areas of discipline. Finally, the larger the class, the greater the scope of networking opportunities. When you leave a larger business school program, you will know individuals at many of the leading national and international corporations—relationships which may prove invaluable to you later in your career. These contacts, however, are only as good as the relationships they are built on. As noted previously, the smaller programs can be more conducive to building tighter relationships, but a lot of this depends on how small the larger programs' sections are.

Ultimately, after reflecting on the factors most important to you, choose the atmosphere that suits you best. You may feel that a smaller school will provide you with the level of intimacy you want, without sacrificing your other career goals. Conversely, you may yearn to be part of a large international program to begin building business contacts across the globe. The choice is yours. Make it an informed one.

SOCIAL ATMOSPHERE

Each business school has a different reputation for social atmosphere. Some schools are known to be competitive and "cutthroat," while others have the reputation for being highly social, cooperative, and laid-back places. While the rumors about certain business programs—particularly the negative rumors—are often exaggerated, if a school has a reputation for being one way or the other, there is usually some basis for it. Talk to current or former students at each program, or visit the school for a few days. Many times, preconceived notions about a school are based on outdated information that has been perpetuated from year to year, and can be completely refuted by talking to several current students. You should also remember that larger programs benefit from a more diverse social atmosphere because of their size, making it more likely that you will find a social group with which you feel comfortable.

Take the time to learn about the social atmosphere of the schools on your list, and be sure to apply to the schools that are a good fit for your personality.

TEACHING PHILOSOPHY AND ATMOSPHERE

Business school classes are typically taught in one of two styles: the lecture method, or the case-study method. Some programs advocate a method of teaching that is employed by most, if not all professors. Other programs leave teaching style to the discretion of the individual professors. For instance, most classes at the Harvard Business School are taught using the case method, whereby students review and prepare a business case study prior to a class, and then spend the class period breaking it down at the direction of the professor. First-year students are assigned to a seat in a particular classroom, and it is the professors who are the mobile entities, coming in and out of that same classroom to teach their class. Classroom etiquette is quite formal, and cold-calling is standard. At Kellogg, by comparison, professors vary widely in teaching style, class atmospheres vary from formal to casual, and participation is obtained by a variety of methods, from cold-calling, to scheduled days, to straight volunteering.

> "The academic reputation of the top five or ten schools is not that different. I believe you will get the same quality education at these schools, and I also believe that your chances of getting a good job are the same regardless of which top ten school you attend. The differences lie more in teaching style and culture. Kellogg and Stanford are similar, as are Harvard, Wharton, and Chicago. The former focus on teams and collaborative learning. The latter focus more on individual achievement and more technical (math) skills. Pick a school that fits your learning style."
>
> —Kanna

Schools also vary in the amount of emphasis they place on working in groups. Some schools require a lot of group work, having made the determination that learning is fostered in this way, and that working well with others on a team is an important skill worth developing for life in the "real world." Other programs place much less emphasis on groupwork, and focus more on the development of individual business skills and knowledge. If you work well with others and like the interaction, it's likely that you'll favor a school that puts a lot of emphasis on group work. If, on the other hand, you are uncomfortable relying on others or prefer to work individually, you'll want to seek out the programs that take that approach to learning. Either way, you should analyze the schools on your list and determine each school's approach to teaching so that you can choose a school with a philosophy that complements your learning style. Information addressing the specifics of a school's teaching philosophy is often omitted from a school's admissions brochure, so again, current students, professors, and recent alumni of a particular program can prove to be valuable resources in getting this information. Similar to the social atmosphere, the teaching philosophy at a particular school will greatly influence your overall experience. Do not underestimate its importance, and *do your homework!*

RELATIONSHIPS WITH PROFESSORS

How approachable are the professors at a given school? Do students feel comfortable seeking extra help and visiting professors during their office hours? Are professors available to students outside of class? How much time do professors actually make available to students? Are office hours offered by the professors, or just by teaching assistants? What is the school's philosophy regarding the balance of research and teaching? How much time are professors expected to devote to students compared to how much they are expected to devote to their own academic endeavors? Does it feel like professors are more interested in their own work than on teaching their students?

And finally, the biggie: Are professors who are good "teachers" valued by the school—or is the school only concerned with retaining the big-name professors who publish a lot?

There is only one way to get the answers to these critical questions—and that is by seeking out current students or recent graduates from each school on your list and putting these questions to them personally. Trust us. The effort you expend in advance will be worth the payoff.

PLACEMENT RECORDS AND EMPLOYMENT RATES AFTER GRADUATION

This is what it is really all about, isn't it?

The *U.S. News and World Report*'s annual rankings of business school programs include a listing of the employment rates for each school. While many schools find ways to "massage" these numbers to produce more favorable results, the trends these numbers show are, nevertheless, worthy of your attention. Be wary of schools with comparatively low employment rates after graduation, and examine a school's statistics over a number of years to see which way a particular school's employment rates are trending.

"The overall rankings of business schools seem kind of arbitrary to me," Matt muses. "Tuck, which was ranked number one last time by the *Wall Street Journal*, but number sixteen by *Business Week*, had one of the highest, if not the single highest, employment rate at graduation."

In addition to overall employment rates, go deeper into the analysis and examine *where* it is that schools are placing their students, and what *type* of placements a school is making. Are most students from a given school going to Fortune 500 corporations? Or are most of a school's students going to companies you have never heard of? Again, you will need to consider your own personal goals in undertaking this analysis. If your goal is to work at a multinational firm, stick to the business schools with a higher percentage of placements at Fortune 500 companies to better your odds, as these percentages do not fluctuate drastically from year to year.

"When making decisions between the top schools, it comes down to a few things: atmosphere, regional bias, and size. I wanted a very collaborative and supportive school that had a strong and loyal alumni base in New England and was smaller in size, which affects the atmosphere. Tuck fit this model perfectly, so it was the right school for me. I know I would have been happy at other schools of similar size and culture, but I would have had a much harder time getting back into a New England venture capital firm from Chicago or Palo Alto, so in that calculus, regional bias played a big part for me," Matt adds.

Once again, detailed placement information may not be readily available in a school's admissions materials. If you cannot find the information you need, call the placement offices of your top-choice schools and put these questions to them directly. Do your homework up front, and you won't be disappointed later.

REPUTATION WITH EMPLOYERS

If your goal is to pursue a career in management, management consulting, brand management, or investment banking, the reputation of the school you choose to attend will play a particularly important role in your recruiting process. Once again, *U.S. News and World Report* collects "reputation" data from top firms and compiles it in its annual review of business schools. If a particular employer views a particular school's program favorably, the employer will put more resources into recruiting at that school, offer more interview slots, conduct more on-campus events, and generally view students from that school in a more favorable light—and as a result, your chances of winning employment with that firm are substantially increased. Conversely, if a potential employer does not hold your school in particularly high regard, or even if an employer simply has no familiarity with it, you'll be fighting an uphill battle through the whole process, and will have to work that much harder to prove your competencies.

The large Fortune 500 companies have been recruiting M.B.A. graduates for a long time, and the hiring committees at these companies have developed their own opinions about certain business school programs based on the performances of their hires over the years. Like it or not, if your goal is to gain employment at one of these companies, you'll have a much easier time of it if you gain admission to one of the "feeder schools" that these companies look to for new hires. This is not the case with all employers, however.

"A lot of employers perceive the students from the top business school programs to have an attitude—a perception which is often true!" Andy observes. "A graduate of one of these top programs that comes into the workplace with an attitude that he deserves more because he is coming from a top school does a disservice both to himself and his school. I think a lot of very good employers intentionally skip the top programs because of this. Still, there never seems to be a shortage of employers coming to wine and dine the students at the top schools."

The message of this chapter, clearly, is to do your homework and make choices based on your specific circumstances. *Don't* get seduced by a school just because of its name or its rank. "You can push hard for any job you want from any M.B.A. program," Matt suggests. "It takes character and honesty to turn down a bigger 'name' school for the school that you know is right for you. Not everyone has this strength, but it is the right thing to do."

PART-TIME VERSUS FULL-TIME PROGRAMS

So what about doing your M.B.A. part-time, in the evening and on weekends, while continuing your day job? In many cases your company may offer to pay either some or all of the tuition for your degree if you agree to do it part-time while you continue to work for them, and commit to staying on for a number of years after finishing the degree. How do you decide if this arrangement is right for you?

"Most people who opt for a part-time or evening program are older, more tenured professionals," Toby notes. "These people are not necessarily seeking to switch industries or functional areas, but rather, have reached a point in their careers where they need the skill set that an M.B.A. provides in order to advance. For this reason, missing out on the networking, the social aspects of the experience, and the opportunity to do a summer internship are less important."

For those who don't fall into this limited category, the mentors were unanimous in their endorsement of full-time programs over part-time programs.

"At the end of the day, an M.B.A. is an M.B.A. whether you earn it full-time or part-time," Brett says. "Part-time programs are often far more economically viable than their full-time counterparts. The part-time experience, however, is very different. On a typical day, students leave work, attend classes, and then return home. Part-time attendees are not immersed in the business school lifestyle and have much less of an 'experience' than their full-time classmates. There is also far less opportunity for meaningful interaction with classmates. These differences convinced me of the merits of attending a full-time program over a part-time or executive program."

"Personally, I wouldn't bother with a part-time or evening program unless I absolutely needed the degree to advance and taking two years off from whatever I was doing was simply not an option. The experience of spending two years immersed in a full-time academic environment with your classmates is a large part of the education you get in business school, and those who do not get to experience that, really miss out on a lot," Alden adds.

"I think if you can afford it, you get a much fuller experience from a full-time program," Amy agrees.

7

An Investment in Your Future

"If you would know the value of money,
go and try to borrow some."
— BENJAMIN FRANKLIN

FUNDING YOUR BUSINESS SCHOOL EDUCATION

IN 2002, the average annual out-of-state tuition at the top fifty–ranked business schools topped $30,000. Once room and board and the cost of books and other expenses are factored in, that number tops $40,000 per year. With a two-year price tag of more than $80,000, business school is no cheap date. You probably don't ordinarily go out and blow eighty grand on a whim, and since, if you're like most people, you probably still have at least some undergraduate debt left on your plate, you should take some time to figure out how exactly it is that you plan to pay for business school.

State schools can be dramatically cheaper if you qualify as an in-state applicant. Not all state schools are created equally, of course, so before you start forum-shopping for a new state in which to establish residency, weigh the savings over time against the quality of education you'll receive, the networking opportunities you'll have, and the reputation of the programs you're considering. It may not be worth it to·attend an in-state program if— after doing your research and consulting the school's placement numbers—you discover that the program, although considerably cheaper, isn't going to get you where you want to go, long-term, in the business world.

Sources of Funding

There are a number of sources of funds for prospective business school students. Absent a personal fortune or a benevolent relative, your funds for tuition and expenses will likely come in the form of loans, grants, scholarships, fellowships, or a combination of these.

In general, financial aid can be divided into three categories: (1) gift aid, (2) student loans, and (3) work-study jobs. Gift aid, such as grants or scholarships, is clearly the best type of financial aid to receive, for, as the name implies, it does not require you to pay it back. Unlike the good ol' days when you were applying to college, however, gift aid is much more limited when applying to business school. Student loans do require you to pay the money back, but are widely available at favorable interest rates, and almost anyone with a decent credit rating can qualify to borrow money under these programs. Work-study jobs are disfavored, because they take precious time away from your business school experience and force you to divide your focus.

"I would recommend financing as much as possible with debt," Andy advises. "The money is cheap and can be paid back over several years. I took the maximum of federal debt [Stafford and Perkins] and funded the balance with university loans, grants, and personal funds. All in all, I think I took out about $80,000 in loans. Needless to say, I didn't have much liquidity when I graduated. It will take some time to realize the full benefit, but in the grand scheme of things, it was worth every penny to me."

Brett agrees: "I took on approximately $100,000 in debt to fund my M.B.A. While I managed to save a good deal of money during my six years between undergrad and grad school, I did not touch my savings and instead opted to take out low-interest academic loans [e.g., Stafford loans]."

The best sources of information about securing funds for business school are the financial aid offices of the individual schools to which you are applying. Each school will have a different relationship with the federal government loan programs, and different scholarship capacities, depending on the size of their endowments and how they choose to allocate funds from it. Contact the financial aid offices of each school as soon as you have decided to apply. Most schools, in addition to the boilerplate federal forms, will require you to complete their own financial aid data forms as well. The earlier your financial aid file at a school is complete, the earlier the school can act on your application, and the better your chances that a school will have remaining money available in scholarships and grants.

Do not procrastinate! In this case, especially, time *is* money.

Federal Financial Aid

The U.S. Department of Education has created the FAFSA (Free Application for Federal Student Aid) to determine individuals' eligibility for the federal student assistance programs. Each year, the FAFSA form is made publicly available in November or December. You can obtain a paper version of the FAFSA application from school financial aid offices, or you can download it from the government website at http://www.fafsa.ed.gov. FAFSA Express software, which allows you to transmit the application electronically, is also available. The FAFSA can be submitted anytime after January 1 of the year you intend to begin school. Send it in as soon as possible for priority consideration.

Plan to file your personal income-tax return early in the year you apply to business schools, in order to make filling out your FAFSA easier, since you will need your total income figures to calculate your Expected Family Contribution (EFC) on the FAFSA form. The EFC is the amount of money an individual and his or her family is "expected" to be able to contribute to the individual's education in a given year. This figure is calculated even if your parents have no intention of contributing *anything* to your tuition. Accordingly, when preparing your taxes, it will inure to your advantage to try to minimize your total income (all items above line 33 on your income tax return), because doing so will reduce your EFC, and thus increase the amount of financial aid you will qualify for. There are several ways you can manage your income to facilitate this, including the following:

- Defer your bonus to the next tax year
- Explain income abnormalities—if you've had a banner year and earned considerably more than you generally do in an average year, make the financial aid office of each school you apply to aware of this anomaly in writing. Include previous tax returns to make your case.
- Become an independent contractor—this may entitle you to write off business expenses above line 33 on your tax return, reducing your total income.
- Avoid incurring capital gains—avoid taking profits on appreciating assets in the year prior to applying for financial aid, and during the years you are in school, as doing so will inflate your income. If you need liquidity, investigate the option of taking out a loan against the value of your assets rather than selling them.

Note that we are neither tax lawyers nor financial advisors. As always, you should see a tax preparer or financial advisor to help you *legally* minimize your personal income.

Most state schools use the Federal Methodology in determining an individual's eligibility for financial aid. This method bases its estimate of your EFC, and ultimately the amount of reduced-interest aid you qualify for on your statement of personal income, assets, and financial liabilities. Private universities, on the other hand, also use the Institutional Methodology to evaluate financial aid eligibility for funds under the school's direct control (unsubsidized loans, grants, and scholarships). Be prepared to fill out additional profile forms if you are applying to private business schools.

When providing this additional information, you may find that some schools still require information about your parents' income. Note that *you are required to provide this information even if your parents will not be making any contibution to your tuition.* Many students mistakenly assume that since their parents are not going to be contributing to their tuition, they do not need to fill out these additional profile forms. This is incorrect! Failing to complete *all* financial aid forms sent to you will result in your financial aid application remaining incomplete, and your being disqualified from receiving any aid award. Even if you think you have filed all of the necessary paperwork with the schools on your list, it is always a good idea to call each school's financial aid office and confirm that they consider your financial aid application complete.

When you begin to hear back from schools, do not be surprised if you receive a wide array of disparate aid packages. Each school has different methods of determining eligibility and different grant and scholarship capacities. Use the best of the financial aid packages you received to leverage the schools that have given you less desirable packages. Don't be obnoxious, but do call the financial aid office and speak to the financial aid officer in charge of your file. Explain your situation, express your preference to attend that school over the school that offered you the better aid package, and *politely* ask if they would reconsider your aid award. The earlier you make this call, the better the chance you can convince a financial aid officer to sweeten your till.

Federal Loans

Federal loan programs view graduate school applicants as independents. Even if you are still living with your parents when you apply to business school, the federal loan program still considers you an independent adult. Only the *federal* financial aid portion of a financial aid package assumes your financial independence from your parents (which usually inures to your advantage). The rest of your aid package can and usually does depend on an independent evaluation by individual schools on your parents' ability to contribute to your education, even if they have no intention of actually doing so! As such, the following discussion of federal loan programs may be of increased importance to you.

Stafford loans (formerly the "guaranteed student loan")

There are two types of Stafford loans: subsidized (need-based) and unsubsidized (not need-based). The differences in these two types of Stafford loans are broken down in the chart below.

	SUBSIDIZED STAFFORD	UNSUBSIDIZED STAFFORD
Maximum amount you can borrow: (1) annually (2) in aggregate	(1) $8,500 (2) $65,000*	(1) $18,500 (2) $138,500
Interest rate**:	Variable; capped at 8.25%.	Variable; capped at 8.25%.
Interest due:	None until you begin repayment schedule (*see below*).	Interest must be paid off each month or it will be added to the principal balance of the loan.
Guarantee fee for loan:	None.	None.

	SUBSIDIZED STAFFORD	UNSUBSIDIZED STAFFORD
Origination fee for loan:	3% up front, but deducted from the balance of the loan amount.	3% up front, but deducted from the balance of the loan amount.
Disbursement:	In two (2) installments, generally, and sent directly to the school. Extra loan proceeds over cost of tuition are paid to you directly or credited to your student account.	In two (2) installments, generally, and sent directly to the school. Extra loan proceeds over cost of tuition are paid to you directly or credited to your student account.
Cancelable?	Yes***.	Yes***.
Repayment schedule:	Standard is ten (10) years. Begins six (6) months after graduation. Extensions are available by authorized deferrals or by consolidating loans.	Standard is ten (10) years. Begins six (6) months after graduation. Extensions are available by authorized deferrals or by consolidating loans.
Repayment plans:	*Standard:* Requires a fixed amount per month with a minimum of $50 per month or the monthly interest accrued, whichever is higher. *Graduated:* Lower payments at first that increase over time. Minimum payments must equal monthly interest accrued.	*Standard:* Requires a fixed amount per month with a minimum of $50 per month or the monthly interest accrued, whichever is higher. *Graduated:* Lower payments at first that increase over time. Minimum payments must equal monthly interest accrued.

SUBSIDIZED STAFFORD	UNSUBSIDIZED STAFFORD
Income-sensitive: Bases monthly payment on a formula including your annual income and the loan amount.	*Income-sensitive:* Bases monthly payment on a formula including your annual income and the loan amount.

*If both subsidized and unsubsidized loans are taken, subsidized loans cannot exceed their maximum of $8,500 per year, and $65,000 in aggregate. Unsubsidized loans may then be stacked over the subsidized loans to their own limits listed in column 2. Subsidized loan aggregate limit includes loans used for undergraduate study.

**Based on the 91-day T-bill rate + 1.7% during school with an additional 0.6% increase after graduation.

***After your school notifies you that it has credited the loan to your account, you many cancel your loan within 14 days or by the first day of the payment period, whichever is later.

In order to be eligible for either of these Stafford loans, you must be enrolled at least half-time in an eligible program of study. Schools administer these loans either through the government's Direct Lending Program, or through banks and other private lenders.

Perkins loan (formerly the "national direct student loan")

The Perkins Loan is offered by participating business schools and, like the subsidized Stafford Loan, is based on need. School financial aid offices use the FAFSA to evaluate student eligibility for the Perkins Loan. Currently, the interest rate on the Perkins Loan is 5 percent, and all interest is paid by the government during the period of your education. Repayment obligations begin nine months after graduation. The maximum annual distribution under a Perkins Loan is $6,000, and the maximum aggregate distribution is $40,000. When repayment obligations begin, students are responsible for repaying the school, as it is the school that is acting as the lender on these loans (with funds contributed by the U.S. government).

The Perkins Loan is extremely favorable due to the government-subsidized interest while you are in school, and very low interest rate.

To learn more about federal loan programs and for the most up-to-date information on rates and program changes, research these programs on the Web at http://www.ed.gov or call the Federal Student Aid Information Center toll-free at 1-800-4-FED-AID (1-800-433-3243). You can also use this number to check on whether your FAFSA has been received and processed by the government.

Private Loans

Private loans are personal loans from a bank or private lending institution. Of all the ways to finance your business school education, private loans are the most expensive, as they generally carry much higher interest rates and will come with a number of extra charges and insurance fees. Just as with unsubsidized federal loans, interest on private loans accrues during school.

If you must take out a private loan to bridge a financial gap between your expenses and your aid package, do everything you can to reduce the overall cost of these loans by shopping around extensively to find and secure the lowest possible interest rate. Having a co-signer on the loan or securing the loan with personal assets will reduce the bank's risk and may persuade a bank to lower its interest rate for you. If your family, or the company you presently work for, maintains a special relationship with a particular bank, that bank may be willing to give you a special rate. You will have to, and should, negotiate these points with a bank to determine the degree of flexibility they have with their rates. The overall cost to you of even a quarter of a point on an interest rate can be extremely significant over time, so make the effort to shop around, and bargain hard for the best deal you can find.

When you begin your negotiation with a bank regarding a personal loan, there are a number of variables to consider, all or many of which can be bargaining chips in that negotiation. In addition, information or concessions you receive at one bank can and should be used to negotiate with the others. Be sure to determine and negotiate the following:

- The interest rate, and how it is determined.
- Whether the interest rate is variable or fixed, and whether the rate is capped.
- Whether the loan can be paid off early without penalty.
- What the term of the loan is (how long you have to pay it off).
- Whether the loan has origination fees, and whether these can be waived.
- Whether the bank requires a co-signer, and whether having one can reduce your interest rate due to the decreased risk to the bank.
- Whether the loan needs to be secured with collateral and whether doing so would reduce your interest rate.
- Whether interest on the loan is tax-deductible.

Once again, making an appointment with a tax planner or a financial advisor can bring benefits here. There may be tax advantages to structuring loans in certain ways, or in taking certain types of loans depending on your personal circumstances. Taking advantage of these tax breaks can bring significant savings over time, so don't blow this off.

Tuition Paid or Reimbursed by an Employer

Ah, yes. Then there is the modern-day incarnation of indentured servitude. Some employers will pay your tuition and expenses if you attend a part-time or evening program while working; while others will pay for full-time attendance in exchange for a promise that you will return to the company and work for a fixed number of years after completing your M.B.A. These arrangements, usually called "leave of absence contracts," however, really do commit you to several years of employment once you return to the company unless you buy your way out with interest and penalties—and, remember that if you change your mind after the fact, there are no federal loan programs or scholarships to help you out. As such, be certain to weigh the financial savings of these arrangements against the significant loss of flexibility in determining the direction of your career; be *extremely* cautious before agreeing to be bound by one; and be certain to read the fine print of the contract so you'll know what the rules are. Generally, these programs are only for individuals who know definitively that they want to be with one particular company long-term and are almost certain not to be swayed from that path during business school.

"Had I wanted to return to Merck for several years after business school, I would have been able to arrange for at least partial funding of my degree. I very much wanted to switch industries after business school, however, so I chose not to solicit Merck's financial assistance," Brett notes. "Several of my classmates did make such arrangements, and were able to do so *only* as a result of their having been identified as 'high potential' employees by their respective firms."

Finally, in booming economic times, you may encounter "angels"—prospective employers that attempt to woo you with offers to help pay off your student loans and other debt, either directly, or in the form of a large signing bonus that can be used for that purpose. "Some companies, particularly consulting firms and investment banks, may offer summer interns who choose to return on a full-time basis an additional bonus that is meant to cover tuition costs," Toby says. Although angels do exist, and in some years are commonplace, changes in the economy or in the economic health of a particular company can make these angels disappear in the blink of an eye. Do not bank on finding an angel to bail you out, however, when planning your financial road to business school. All it takes is one bad financial quarter to change the landscape within a company. As such, until such an arrangement is signed, sealed, and delivered, don't count on it.

Grants and Scholarships

Financial grants are awarded based on need and, generally, only after all other forms of aid have been maxed out. In making these awards, financial aid officers typically focus on those students who have exhausted their federal Stafford and Perkins Loan eligibility, in order to help get these students "over the hump" in satisfying their unfunded education expenses.

Scholarships, by contrast, may be awarded based on need, or simply on merit to award outstanding achievement. Most business school scholarships award academic excellence, but some also recognize other things like a high level of commitment to community service. Many schools have particular scholarships set up by alumni to recognize traits or qualities that those alumni found meaningful. To learn more about the specific grant and scholarship programs available at the schools you intend to apply to, contact each school's financial aid offices.

Oh, and during your conversations with financial aid officers, don't be shy about asking for each school's statistics regarding the percentage of the student body that receives some type of financial aid, the percentage of the student body receiving grants and scholarships directly from the school, and the average of each of these awards per student.

Finally, private grants and scholarships are also offered by a host of other institutions, businesses, and organizations. Devote some time to surfing the Web or researching in the library to identify these sources. One such source, which claims to have a database of over 10,000 grants and scholarships in all areas of academia, is http://www.absolutelyscholarships.com.

The Federal Work-Study Program

The Federal Work-Study Program arranges employment for students who need additional funding to bridge gaps in financing their education. Awards are granted based on need, and the total amount of an award is determined by several factors, including (1) when a student applies for the program; (2) the student's level of need; and (3) the funding provided by the student's school.

Once an award is made, a work schedule is determined by each individual student's total financial aid package, class schedule, and academic progress. Students are guaranteed at least minimum wage, and often higher, based on their skill sets and experience. Schools pay the student directly and must do so at least once a month, or, if authorized to do so by the student, the school can credit a bank loan or any institutional charges such as tuition, room and board, and other fees.

PAYING IT OFF

Although this chapter is about finding and arranging the funding for your business school education, it is never too early to consider how you plan to pay off your debts after graduation. Outstanding loans can easily begin to influence career decisions. Nobody likes the feeling of lugging around a huge debt burden, and the temptation to pay it off as soon as possible may cause you to change or adjust your career goals.

Once you are in the middle of the experience, you may find yourself drifting away from your original post–business school career goals and being drawn toward the higher-paying jobs. These feelings may be related to a genuine change in career objectives, but many times the change is actually motivated by money and a desire to pay off debt burdens as fast as possible in order to "get on with life."

While debt is uncomfortable, it is preferable to selling yourself out and settling for a life other than the one you designed for yourself. Determine whether a temporary detour for a several-year tour of duty at a high-paying job in a consulting firm or an investment bank in the name of debt relief will still allow you to find your way back to your chosen career path. If you conclude that it will, set some clear financial goals, force yourself to save money and reduce your debt, and plan your exit strategy and your route back to your goal. Many, many graduates find themselves seduced by high-dollar offers, get hooked on the lifestyle associated with these high-stress, high-paying jobs, and never actually make it back to the original plan they had for their lives.

Sure, some people find satisfaction and happiness in this change of plans. Many others, however, simply become victims of inertia, and don't recognize the abandonment of their professional goals and dreams until it all comes apart in a midlife crisis. Don't let a temporary debt burden frighten you into making bad decisions that will negatively impact your life. If you have followed the advice in this book so far, you are going to business school for a clearly defined purpose and with some clearly defined career goals in mind.

Keep your eye on the ball!

8

The Things to Do Before Classes Begin

"Spectacular achievement is always preceded
by spectacular preparation."
— ROBERT H. SCHULLER

A T SOME POINT in the weeks before you conclude your affairs, pack up your belongings, and head off to business school, you'll begin to be pestered by a nagging feeling that you should be "doing something" to prepare yourself for the experience. If you have this book in hand and actually finish it, you will be a lot more prepared for what's to come than most of your classmates. Still, there are a handful of things you *should* do before business school begins to assure that you arrive prepared and ready to hit the ground running.

Notify your present employer of your departure date.

While this advice seems obvious, a lot of people either intentionally or purposefully burn bridges by failing to give their employers proper notice before they depart for business school. Some make last-minute plans to join friends or family on an extended summer vacation. Others are so fed up with their jobs, their boss, or their company, that they just quit whenever they feel like it.

No matter how frustrated you may be in your current position, *don't* do this.

Unless you get into only one business school and you get in off the waitlist, you should have your plans in place sometime during the spring. Once you've made the decision to matriculate, inform your current employer of your intended departure date in a friendly and amicable way. Doing this will ensure that you have enough time to wrap up or transition any ongoing projects, and that your employer will be able to plan for a seamless transition of workflow and responsibility in anticipation of your departure.

Taking the time to do this is your professional responsibility, and will ensure that you leave on good terms. Remember that circumstances change, and people talk. You never know where your old colleagues may end up.

As you prepare to depart, remember to sign up for COBRA[1] or to transfer onto your spouse's health-care plan. Even if there are only a few weeks, or even days, between your last day of employment coverage and your first day of university coverage, and even though COBRA gap coverage can be expensive, don't gamble. The last thing you need is to get sick or injured on vacation and to not have health insurance.

Speaking of vacation . . .

There are two schools of thought about how to spend the summer before you begin business school. The first view is that this summer presents you your last extended opportunity to travel, see the world, or engage your hobbies before you enter or reenter the

---

[1]COBRA, the Consolidated Omnibus Budget Reconciliation Act of 1985, is a federal statute that requires most employers with group health plans to permit employees the opportunity to temporarily continue their group health coverage, for a fee, under the employer's plan after leaving the company.

business world full-time. The opposing position is that the summer before business school represents three additional months of income that you could use to reduce your debt burden and potentially provide yourself with greater flexibility, or more options on the other end. Not surprisingly, your mentors have strong opinions on the subject.

"I was pretty lame," Brett admits. "I finished up work on a Wednesday, and started business school one week later. My biggest concern upon entering business school was money or, should I say, the lack thereof. As such, I elected to work for as long as I could. If I had it to do all over again, I would have traveled instead."

"I spent the summer in Peru taking 'business Spanish' courses at a business school in Lima and traveling around the country. I also took a ski trip to Chile in late July. It was awesome," Dave recalls.

"Travel, travel, travel!" Kanna implores.

"I got married and took an extended honeymoon," Matt remembers. "I wish I could do it all over again! Whatever you do, definitely take some time off and if you can, do something you have always wanted to do—travel, volunteer, whatever. It may be the last chance you get to do this sort of thing for a while."

"I worked through July and spent the balance courting my girlfriend (now my wife!). If I were to do it all over again . . . I mean, in the event I wasn't courting . . . I would definitely travel and enjoy the time off," Andy teases. "I know it is hard to do, considering the large financial burden you are taking on, but in the end, it's all relative. What's another few thousand dollars in the grand scheme of things, right? For most, this will be the last time for a long while that one can take a month off and see the world. Do it!"

Whatever option you choose, try to, at a minimum, take two or three weeks off before you begin school to rest up, recover, and get ready for school. You want to start the program energized, refreshed, and ready to go—not tired and run-down from whatever it was you just left behind.

Many business school programs offer adventure trips as a sort of "bonding experience" for incoming students in the week before school officially begins. These trips provide a great opportunity to meet and get to know some of your future classmates in a relaxed, noncompetitive setting. These programs generally earn rave reviews, and the friendships that crystallize during these trips can provide you with immediate project partners and networks throughout your business school experience, and friends and contacts for a lifetime. These programs are not just "for the kids." *Go.*

Confirm your financing arrangements.

The previous chapter outlined the many different sources of financing available to help you pay for business school. By early summer, you should have a good idea which of these sources or combination of sources you are going to use. Though you won't start classes until the fall, lining up and confirming your financing arrangements will give you the flexibility to make changes in those plans, if necessary, and will also provide you with the peace of mind that comes from knowing that you have your financial house in order so you can relax and enjoy the end of the summer.

Have all of your paperwork and confirmations together in a file or series of files, and take these files with you to business school. That way, if a problem arises, resolving that problem can occur with a minimum of time, effort, and disruption.

Arrange for housing.

In late spring, you should also begin making the necessary arrangements for your relocation. Often this involves finding an apartment in a new city.

When searching for an apartment in any major metropolitan area, and especially near a university campus, your best bet is to start looking early—before the spring crop of students graduates in May. Enlist the help of a current student or friend who already lives in the city where you'll be landing. Current students have typically done their homework on the housing market and usually have the "inside scoop" on which apartment buildings have the best management, the best rents, and the best amenities, and can also often put you in touch with someone whose apartment will be coming available. As with all housing choices, there are several areas of concern worth remembering as you select your housing for business school.

First, if you are moving to a major metropolitan area, you need to find out what areas of town are considered "safe" for students who keep odd hours; which housing complexes are the most convenient to campus; and which ones offer the best amenities. While safety is always paramount, convenience and proximity to campus are also very important during your time at business school. You will have countless group meetings and projects requiring you to be at school at all hours of the day and night and on all days of the week. Picking a complex within safe walking distance from campus, or at least proximate to safe public transportation that runs seven days a week, is very helpful. An apartment close to campus will also give you the flexibility to go back and forth from home during the day.

So what about the dorms? you ask.

If dorms are available to business school students, these would seem to satisfy all of the criteria we have just listed. But don't just jump right in and sign your university's graduate-school dorm lease. First, ask a student whether the dorms are livable, both aesthetically and socially, and how the rents compare to comparable rents for nearby apartments. Often, universities charge a *huge* premium for dorm space, capitalizing on students who are either too lazy or too unfamiliar with the area around campus to make their own housing decisions.

Dorms can, however, be very convenient, as they are generally either on or very close to campus, and tend to be outfitted with a number of student-friendly amenities like computer lab rooms, meeting rooms, copy machines, high-speed Internet access in every room, and community workout and chill-out spaces where you can socialize and unwind. Living in the dorm also puts you in close proximity to your classmates, which can facilitate meetings, groupwork, and socializing and bonding.

"Since group projects are such a large component of school, I think it makes sense to be close to everyone," Andy advises.

"I would recommend doing whatever the majority of folks do because that enables you to be a part of the 'scene' more readily," Alden agrees.

"To get the most out of the nonacademic aspects of business school, I recommend following the herd, too," Brett notes. "Do whatever is most common at the school in question to facilitate your social interactions outside the classroom. Business school is more than just classes and recruiting. It's an experience. If you're not constantly around your classmates, you're going to miss out on key opportunities to learn about people, their interests, and their aspirations. I often felt sorry for my classmates who lived out in the suburbs, because they were missing out on a lot."

On the other hand, living in the dorm puts you in close proximity to your classmates *all the time*, which can facilitate stress, frustration, and claustrophobia. Business school dorm life is *not* the same party scene you remember from your college days. Most nights are spent working, and when you spend so much time with the same people in such close proximity, little foibles, personality quirks, and annoying habits can quickly become major issues. Consider whether spending all day with your classmates and then going home and seeing the same people in the gym, the laundry, and the rec room will be too overwhelming.

What about roommates?

Be wary of taking on a roommate in business school, whether you are in a dorm or in an off-campus apartment, even if that roommate is a compatible old friend living and working in the city you're going to, or studying there in another graduate program. The last thing you need in business school is a clash of schedules, conflicting work or sleep habits, someone with annoying habits, or the lure of a friend to tempt you away from your work. You are in professional school, with a limited time to make the most of the experience. Do what you can to maximize your chances of staying focused on the goal.

"I moved in with two classmates from school to an off-campus house and really enjoyed it," Amy recalls. "I originally wanted to live alone, but it worked out, particularly in the first year, to live with people who were doing the same thing that I was. We were able to figure it out together and have a great time!"

"Roommates can be good if they have the same work ethic. They can be a great influence if you can work together and motivate one another to excel. If your roommates prefer the social element of school, however, you can be tempted to the bars more than the books," Andy warns.

"Yeah, I haven't had a roommate in several years, and I had

no plans to switch back," Dave adds. "I suggest doing what makes you comfortable. I suggest living off campus but near the school. You don't want to feel imprisoned, but you also don't want to spend a lot of time commuting between classes. Be careful if your roommate is not in the business program—you run the risk of very conflicting schedules."

Important considerations for your living space.

One of the most important things to look for in business school housing, other than location, is having enough space—especially separate areas to study and sleep. You will be doing a lot of work at home, spending a lot of time researching and gathering information and data on the Internet, and communicating back and forth with classmates by e-mail. Given the prominent role the Internet and e-mail will play in your everyday life in business school, look for an apartment that offers high-speed Internet access, or at least has the necessary wiring to enable you to access it. You will be exchanging a lot of documents with groupmates late into the night, and waiting forty-five minutes for a document to download at two A.M. can be very frustrating. Pay the extra dollars to assure yourself of access to technology.

In case you haven't gleaned this yet, with all the hard work and late hours you'll be keeping, sleep will be at a premium.

When your day's work is done, it is psychologically important to be able to physically distance yourself from your work to help yourself mentally shut down for the night. As such, the importance of having enough space to accomplish this and to enable yourself to live comfortably should not be underestimated. Trade in your old, beat-up futon for a real bed with a real mattress, and make your bedroom conducive to relaxation. Oh, and before you sign a lease, verify that the area around your apartment building is quiet at night. Having both lived in the same building over a bar in New Haven known for its rowdy crowds and reliable nightly fights and police intervention, we speak from experience.

Use the summer to get in shape.

No, we're not kidding. The long hours of reading and thinking that you'll be doing in business school require stamina. A routine daily workout can refresh you, clear your mind, keep you awake and alert, and make your days more productive. Of course, you don't want to have to deal with the soreness and adjustment associated with a new workout program once business school begins, and you'll want to capitalize on the many benefits of being in shape from the first day anyway—so start now! Begin a physical workout program no later than June or July to increase your fitness so that it will become a regular part of your routine and easy to continue once business school begins. Almost all of us made time in our daily schedules to run, blade, bike, shoot hoops, play tennis or squash, or participate in aerobics. Having this little oasis in an otherwise crowded day can really make a difference.

Check in with the registrar.

You'll be thanking us out loud for this piece of advice.

Among the piles of paperwork you'll receive during the summer before business school will be a form from the Registrar's Office. It's standard issue at just about every educational institution nowadays, and chances are you'll remember running around with your parents trying to track everything down for the one you filled out for college. On it, you'll have to provide a complete, updated list of your vaccinations, medications, and any health conditions your school should know about. Many schools will also ask for a copy of your Social Security card and/or birth certificate for your file. During the course of your business school career, you'll need many other "important papers" as well, so here's a timesaver that will spare you copious amounts of frustration later.

Get yourself a folder—and, if possible, pick one that is brightly colored so you'll never misplace it. In it, place one copy each of (1) your birth certificate; (2) Social Security card; (3) medical history, including a complete and updated history of all inoculations; (4) driver's license or state-issued ID card; (5) three certified copies of your undergraduate transcript (you'll need to request this in writing from the Registrar at your undergraduate institution and pay a small fee for it); (6) one uncertified photocopy of your undergraduate transcript (which, obviously, you can make by photocopying one of the certified copies); (7) one certified and one uncertified copy of a transcript for each graduate degree you carry, if any; (8) one photocopy of each of your undergraduate and graduate diplomas; and (9) your original, current passport.

Some of these items, like your medical history and two forms of identification, will be required before you are allowed to register for classes. Others, like certified copies of your undergraduate transcript, may or may not be required to matriculate, but will certainly be required by employers during employment recruiting. You'll probably need copies of your undergraduate diploma in order to graduate. As for the passport, more than one person we know had a partner come into his or her office during a summer internship and say, "I need you to fly to London with me to help with such and such project. We'll be leaving on Wednesday."

Don't be the schmoe who can't go on the trip because you don't have a current passport. Renew it now, put it in the folder, and forget about it.

Read now, sign up later.

If your business school is anything like ours, beginning in late May or early June, you'll start getting inundated with mailings, pamphlets, and brochures. There was the pickup-and-deliver weekly laundry service; the weekly dorm-room linen service; the "buy now and save" offers; and the offers for meal plans and "exclusive," graduate student–only "dining clubs." The campus computer center was urging you to buy a computer. In fact, everyone seemed to be hocking something. So how do you wade through this blizzard of materials and separate the necessary from the wasteful? How do you know what you need?

It's really quite simple. As each of these "Act now!" offers comes in, log them in on a list, throw the brochures and order forms into a big manila envelope, and wait. You can buy later. Here's a little secret: Almost all of these ". . . but you must act now!" offers miraculously reappear for "one week only" during the first week or two of classes.

Once you get to campus, talk to your upperclass mentor or other second-year students about the various items on your list. Scope out the typical patterns of behavior and *then* buy. Other than a computer (*see below*) which may be offered at an unbeatable price, there is nothing that these organizations are selling that can't wait until you arrive on campus. The last thing you want to do is sink two thousand dollars into the "prestigious graduate-only dining room" only to discover that it is a long, inconvenient walk from the business school that no other students make, and that you have just condemned yourself to three meals a day with three dorks from the physics lab and a horde of arrogant and aggressive law students. Remember the simple lesson of this section: Read now, buy later. It will save you much money and aggravation.

Get outfitted with a good IBM-compatible laptop computer.

You need a laptop computer in business school. Some schools require you to buy a particular brand preloaded with the software packages you'll need for your coursework. Other schools may simply require that you have certain software and networking capabilities. Watch closely the materials that your school sends you and follow the requirements so you don't end up with the wrong technology.

Schedule your move-in time at least six weeks in advance.

If you are moving into an apartment for the first time, you may not know that many apartment complexes will not allow you to move your belongings in the passenger elevators. There are freight elevators for this purpose—and they are booked in advance by your building's management office. Don't make the mistake of arriving with your U-Haul full of your earthly belongings without a move-in time and elevator appointment unless you like sleeping in trucks.

If you aren't sure whether you need a move-in appointment, it's a simple matter to call your landlord or the management office of your building and ask. Make this call at least six weeks in advance of the date you hope to move in, to assure that you'll have access to an elevator.

AFTER YOU'VE ARRIVED ON CAMPUS

Set up headquarters.

The first task deserving of your attention when you arrive in town before business school starts is setting up your living quarters and your "office." As stated previously, your apartment will need to serve multiple purposes. You need a quiet, uncluttered and well-organized place to study, an area to entertain friends or your work groups, and a place to escape from everything—books, friends, and classmates included. Don't forget that it often takes several days to get Internet access, phone service, and cable television installation appointments—and you'll need at least the phone and Internet immediately—so don't arrive in town twenty-four hours before school activities begin unless you are a masochist and enjoy scheduling yourself into conflicts. Three or four days of lead time is generally sufficient. If you're lucky, your landlord might be able to handle these arrangements for you—so don't forget to ask!

As to the setup itself, your study area should include a strong desk with enough space for your computer and peripherals (printer, fax machine, et cetera) and enough additional space for you to spread out your reading materials. Other study-area items should include a file cabinet, a comfortable chair for longer reading assignments, high-speed Internet access *at your desk*, and a sturdy door to separate your study area from any roommates. Again, remember that furniture takes time to be delivered, and if you live in a high-rise, you need to schedule delivery times with the office to assure that the freight elevator will be available—so if you're buying your bed and desk new, don't leave this for the last minute.

Get to know the lay of the land.

After you've moved in, give yourself at least a couple of days to get to know your neighborhood and work out your routine. Figure out what gym you're going to join, where you're going to buy your groceries, where you're going to get your morning coffee, and where the major chain stores are. Learn the public transportation system. And take an afternoon to familiarize yourself with the campus. As we mentioned earlier, it will make your life a lot easier if you plan the end of your summer to allow you to do these things.

Update your résumé.

Recruiting for first-year summer jobs starts almost as soon as you start classes. At most schools, this process is overseen by the career management center. As soon as you are able, check in with the career management office. Introduce yourself to the staff, and borrow any materials or publications they provide on how to structure and streamline your résumé. Do not assume that you already know how to structure a résumé, and that any advice the center could provide would be intuitive. If it was, the knowledgeable and savvy people running the career development offices at the top business schools in the country wouldn't bother to provide the resource. You're in business school to learn. Take advantage of every resource offered to you.

In the unlikely event that your school's career management center does not offer a résumé workshop or consultation service, you'll need to update your résumé on your own. The last time you worked on your résumé, you were probably preparing to send it as part of your business school applications. Do not use the same version to send to employers! Bring it current. Add your candidacy for an M.B.A., the school and program you are attending, an expected completion date, and any work-related accomplishments you may have achieved since applying to business school. Be certain that your résumé includes a good description of your employment experience, taking care to show your progression through the ranks of the company or companies for which you worked. Do not leave unexplained gaps in the years between college and your application to business school. You will, no doubt, see ways to revise the description of your accomplishments and work experience based on your review of the materials from the career center. You may even want to prepare several different versions of your résumé, each targeted to different industries.

Remember, your résumé is your calling card. It is the first impression potential employers will get—and if it isn't perfect, it may be the *only* impression they get. Take the time to get it right.

Get a local cell phone.

A cell phone is now standard equipment in business school, as it is in the business world, and there are several good reasons why you should get one and learn how to operate its features. First, you'll want to be reachable by any and all potential employers at all times. If you have group meetings or classes all day, or are working in the library or a study room at school, a cell phone will allow you to excuse yourself and answer an important call immediately, or at least enable you to return calls between meetings or classes.

Furthermore, if you have chosen to live with a roommate, cell phone–based voicemail will assure your privacy in your interview invitations, acceptances, and rejections. This can help to avoid competition and/or embarrassment.

A cell phone is also a very useful means of communication with your classmates and groupmates. You will have many group assignments during your business school career, and being able to get in touch with your groupmates quickly and easily to schedule or reschedule meetings, and to pass on information, is critical to your efficiency.

Finally, a cell phone can help you keep in touch with your spouse, family, and friends. Because business school students are very busy and spend very little time at home, a cell phone will allow you to fill five- or ten-minute breaks in your schedule with a quick call to check in with your family. Having a cell phone can help you learn where everyone is planning to go for dinner or drinks, or where you can meet up with people after your obligations for the day end.

For better or for worse, cell phones are now an important tool in the business world. Being both familiar with and fluent in the use of technology is an important, if not essential, requirement. While it is not necessary to have every high-tech gadget available in an effort to impress employers, you *do* want to appear professional and aware of contemporary business standards.

Buy your books early and find out if there are any assignments for the first day of classes.

Your first-semester classes in business school are typically mostly or all required "core" classes. As a result, almost every other incoming first-year student will be trying to get their hands on many of the same books. Determine from the advance materials your school sends you whether it is possible to access your class websites before classes begin, or whether there is an area on your school's intranet that publishes required textbooks for each class. If none of these resources is available, you may also be able to find out directly from the bookstore which textbooks your classes require. Whichever way you can, get your textbooks and course packets as soon as possible. While you might think that a business school–affiliated bookstore would eventually learn how to plan inventory, the bookstore almost *always* sells out of both textbooks and course packets. You don't want to fall behind in your assignments waiting for a second order of books to arrive—so shop early!

Math Camp

Ahh, yes. The age-old business school question. To go, or not to go? Exactly how big a goober will you look like if you decide to go? But can you afford not to go?

If you were not a math or econ major in college, and harbor some reservations about the competence of your math skills, you may find enrolling in this "refresher" program to be quite helpful. Many business schools offer such a program, affectionately known as "math camp," to provide you with renewed instruction on the specific math skills you will need during business school. The program usually lasts no more than a week, and is typically given during the week just prior to the beginning of classes. Taking this ungraded refresher program is a great way to ease yourself back into the academic setting and to help alleviate the significant anxiety that many of us have about math.

Attending math camp will also give you the opportunity to meet many of your new classmates in a relatively relaxed setting before classes officially begin. A huge benefit without significant drawbacks, we recommend math camp to anyone who wasn't a math jock in college.

"Regardless of whether you need it substantively, math camp is your first opportunity to acclimate yourself to school and begin making friends and contacts," Toby points out. "By skipping math camp, you risk missing out on an important social opportunity to bond with your classmates. My closest friends in business school were people I began friendships with during math camp."

"I skipped math camp because I was a math major in undergrad," Brett notes. "In retrospect, however, I shouldn't have been so bold. The material was unique and very much slanted toward business problems, so my undergraduate education really wasn't appropriate preparation. Even if it were, though, I still should have taken part in math camp. The week was a huge party, as I found out after the fact, and took place at a time when business school stress was at a minimum. I was sorry to have missed that."

"Math camp was great," Anne recalls, "but mostly from the perspective of being able to meet people early on. The material was pretty basic, but it never hurts to have a review."

"I went, and I would recommend going even if you don't need to brush up on your math skills," Alden counsels. "The experience of meeting your classmates in a pretty relaxed environment before classes begin, is very valuable and can significantly improve your first-year experience."

Attendance at math camp, and the perception of attendance there, does seem to be somewhat school-specific, however:

"I did not go to math camp, and I don't know anyone who did," Dave recalls.

"Math camp was for suckers," Kanna chuckles. "Everything you need to know you can learn later."

"Yeah, I say skip it unless you are completely unfamiliar with math and Excel," Matt agrees.

Orientation

Business school orientation typically involves a series of mixers and team-building exercises in an effort to get the class to mingle and interact. Though these exercises can feel foolish and silly, they are effective in their purpose. Don't take yourself too seriously: Lighten up, laugh a little, don't be afraid to embarrass yourself, and roll with the exercises. This is where first impressions are made. People are drawn to those who practice a little self-deprecation.

Orientation may also provide you the opportunity to meet some of your professors in a social setting, learn your way around campus, and become acquainted with the second-year students who help to run the orientation—whose friendship and counsel could prove to be invaluable. So resist the urge to blow off orientation. While you will likely experience some ridiculous moments, we think that on balance, orientation is time well spent.

Placement Tests

If you think you have sufficient skills in a particular "core" discipline, you may elect to take a placement test that will allow you to "waive out" of the regular "core" level class. But how do you know whether or not to try and place out, and how many courses you should try to place out of?

"There are three reasons to stay in the core. First, the social element. You get to work with your classmates more and get to know one another in the classroom. Second, you establish the same base of knowledge as your classmates. No matter what undergraduate school one attended, it is highly unlikely that a course was taught at the same level as it will be in business school. Third, especially in the first term, some familiarity with the course material makes it easier to excel," Andy counsels.

"I was an undergraduate business major, and as a result, I waived out of a lot of the first-year course requirements," Toby explains. "In hindsight, I think I placed out of too many classes. I now believe it is important to refresh one's skills even if you have some familiarity with the material. This is particularly important in the more quantitative courses like finance and accounting. Because I didn't take many of the traditional first-year classes, at times I missed references made in upper-level classes to cases or projects covered in the prerequisite courses. That said, you still need to assess your skill level. For example, if you are a CPA, there is clearly no need for you to take Introductory Accounting."

Matt agrees: "If you are truly comfortable with the material, then opt out, since doing so will give you more opportunity to take electives and meet people in the second-year class. I opted to pass out of Micro- and Macroeconomics and Corporate Finance, since I was an economics major in college."

Kanna seems to echo the sentiment favoring placing out of basic courses: "Place out of Statistics, Accounting, and Basic Finance if you are comfortable with those subjects. You don't really need to learn basic math again."

The sign-up period for placement tests is often during the summer, announced by some of the materials you will receive before classes begin. No one is likely to notify you a second or third time about this opportunity, so if you overlooked the sign-up application during the summer, make inquiries about it at the Registrar's Office as soon as you arrive at school. Some schools also offer placement tests to determine in what level of a particular discipline you should be placed. These, too, are offered before classes begin, so keep an eye out for notifications of these opportunities. Given the mild disagreement among the mentors about what to place out of, you might want to check with second-year students at your individual school to determine the best course of action to follow.

9

An Overview of the
Typical First-Year Curriculum

*"Where you come from is not nearly as important as
where you are going."*

—VARIOUS

DURING YOUR FIRST YEAR, you will be required to take courses
included in the *core curriculum* at your particular school, or
demonstrate sufficient proficiency on a placement test administered by your school to waive out of one or more of these required courses. As you might imagine, the first-year curriculum
at most business schools is generally pretty standard—designed
to give you a broad overview and at least a conversational fluency
in each of the general areas commonly encountered in the business world. Yes, even if you plan to spend the rest of your career
in finance as an investment banker, you will have to complete at
least the core courses in marketing and accounting.

Core classes in the first year are likely to include some varia-
tion on the following:

- Marketing Management
- Accounting for Decision-Making
- Strategies for Managing Organizations
- Business Strategy
- Corporate Finance

- Statistical Methods for Management of Decisions
- Microeconomic Analysis
- Operations Management

Business schools require you to achieve proficiency in the core curriculum in order to provide you with an overall understanding of the general business concepts you may encounter in your career, and to develop a common business language. Although you need not (and, within the temporal limits of your business school education, cannot) become an expert in all of these disciplines— after you have completed your core requirements, you should have at least a solid, basic understanding of each. Business schools endeavor to develop managers, and once you reach senior levels of management, you will need to be at least conversationally fluent with all of the divisions of your firm.

Therein lies the purpose of the core curriculum.

Sections

Most schools divide each incoming class into smaller groups, commonly called—you guessed it—"sections." Sections are created for both academic and social reasons. The smaller class sizes they produce facilitate greater interaction among students and the professor, and among fellow students, and thus produce a better-quality learning experience in the classroom. Furthermore, students within each section will have the same class schedule for· at least the first term, and in many schools, the entire first year, which helps to build greater familiarity, friendships, and working relationships. Sections generally range in size between fifty and seventy-five people.

SUBJECTS IN THE CORE CURRICULUM

Marketing management

Marketing Management provides an analytical approach to the various marketing problems faced by firms. This class teaches students the necessary skills to coordinate corporate and marketing objectives, and to make appropriate decisions about production, product positioning and targeting, pricing, promotion, and distribution channels consistent with those objectives.

Accounting for decision-making

Designed for students with little or no experience in accounting, the introductory business school accounting course covers the basics of accounting, focusing on how various economic events are communicated through the financial reporting process. The course will also teach you how to develop, construct, and analyze corporate financial statements.

Strategies for managing organizations

The introductory management course teaches you the basics about how to manage social networks, how to organize and motivate people in the firm, and how to implement strategic change. Among the subjects covered are the expectancy theory of work and reward, negotiation and decision-making techniques, cultural influences on organizations, and group dynamics.

Business strategy

The introductory management and strategy course teaches you the fundamentals of profitability and provides the basic analytical tools for corporate decision-making to produce greater wealth for corporate shareholders. The course typically progresses through many types of analysis, including scope, market, resource, positioning, sustainability, and opportunity. Analysis of the firm's internal value-creating abilities and the influence of external environmental forces will be addressed. Common theories addressed in this class include Porter's Five Forces, Value Net, the Resource-Based View, and Economic Value Creation.

Corporate finance

The introductory finance course in business school addresses the general principles of corporate finance, introducing you to the concepts and techniques necessary to analyze and implement optimal investment decisions for firms. The course typically centers on asset valuation, capital budgeting, the risk-reward relationship, and the impact of access to information on capital budgeting decisions.

Statistical methods for the management of decisions

The required introductory statistics class provides the background competence in statistics needed to analyze common business situations and make strategic decisions based on those analyses. Typical topics include simple subjects like basic probability theory and decision trees, and more sophisticated statistical techniques like regression analysis.

Microeconomic analysis

Business school microeconomics introduces the basic tools of micoeconomic analysis and decision-making as applied within the managerial context. "Micro," as it is often called, addresses topics including consumer theory, demand, production and costs, pricing, perfect competition, monopolies, oligopolies, and game theory.

Operations management

The Operations class is the wild card. An instrumental part of the core curriculum at some business schools, it is not even found at many others. Where offered, Operations Management exposes students to the basic principles of manufacturing operations, teaching you how to model and understand the manufacturing process and how to develop strategies for successfully managing manufacturing operations.

FIRST-YEAR ELECTIVES

If you attend a business school that keeps students in sections with a mandatory core curriculum for the entire first year, feel free to skip ahead to the next part of the chapter . . . but for those of you at schools that disband sections after the first term, or are on the trimester system and offer curriculum choice in the first year, there are some important issues to consider when selecting your second-term, or second- and third-trimester "elective" classes.

The first thing to remember is that this isn't college, and you don't have a comfortable four-year cushion in which to take all of the classes that interest you. As such, your first responsibility is to plot out your remaining required "core" courses, and to figure out where you intend to put those required courses in your schedule during your remaining terms or trimesters. In business school, it is two years and out, and in many cases, certain classes are only offered once a year, or are only taught by a particularly desirable professor once a year. The last thing you want to discover in your final term is that you forgot about a required "core" course, and have to take it with the least desirable professor—or worse yet, that is isn't being offered! Don't lose track of your required courses.

Once you are free of the mandatory schedule, you should also spend some time plotting out the elective classes you hope to take during business school. Determine what, if any, prerequisites those courses have, and endeavor to complete those prerequisites as soon as you are able to provide yourself with maximum flexibility. The most desired elective classes fill up quickly (see "Bidding" section below), and as such, the more flexibility you allow yourself in scheduling your desired courses, the better your chances of being able to take more of the classes and professors you want.

On that subject, you should also spend some time looking at which professors are teaching which classes, and what teaching styles they employ (see "Teaching Philosophies" in Chapter 10). In many cases, you will find that the same class is taught by several different professors, employing different teaching philosophies, imposing different course requirements, and that the courses are being offered at several different times. Don't just leave your experience up to chance! Take some ownership of your experience!

How? Strive to find out which professors have the best reputations in a particular subject area, and why. Your school may have a professor evaluation system set up whereby you can reference each professor's "ratings" on a number of different factors, including teaching ability, personality, difficulty of exams, and so on. Even if your school does have a formal evaluation system like this, though, don't forget to consult second-year students, who can offer the most recent opinions and feedback on professors' styles, the amount of work they assign, their availability, approachability, interest in the subject matter, and more.

Above all, don't underestimate the role the professor plays in your overall experience in a class. The best professors can make even the driest subject matter interesting and memorable, while a horrible professor can make the best classes intolerable. Invest the time to find the professors that suit you best.

Considering a Major

Though you will not have to decide definitively on a major during your first year, it is never too early to consider what discipline(s) interest you most. If you find yourself with the flexibility to enroll in some non-"core" courses during your first year, try to take classes to help inform your decision about a major course of study. Become familiar with the required classes for the major(s) in which you are most interested—a factor which should help to focus your selection of what first-year classes to take to ensure compliance with prerequisites for upper-level coursework.

Again, business school lasts only two brief years. Don't waste even a single course slot. Every course you take should have a purpose.

AN INTRODUCTION TO THE "BIDDING SYSTEM"

Most business schools handle students' selection of elective courses through a capitalistic "bidding system," wherein students have a certain number of units of "currency" they can use to "purchase" slots in elective courses. No two schools use precisely the same system, and every school imposes its own rules about what is and is not allowed, and as such, it is difficult to provide specific advice about how to "game" the bidding system for maximum success.

Some general advice, however, is possible.

First, read the material your school provides you about the course bidding system carefully, and map it out until you understand every aspect of it thoroughly. Once you have mastered the "rules of the road" at your particular school, solicit advice from your upperclass mentor and other trusted second-year students about the hints and tricks they have learned to "beat the system." For every school's "bidding system," there are loopholes and strategies which, if you know them, can maximize your chances of gaining admission to the classes and professors you most desire.

"Wharton's online auction was, in my view, a fun and equitable means of bidding for classes. At the start of business school, I was allotted five thousand 'points' to spend over the course of two years. Each semester, the bidding cycle was comprised of twelve rounds, during which students could buy and sell seats in courses. When you successfully bid on a course, you pay the highest losing bid. When you bid unsuccessfully, you pay nothing. At the end of each semester, you are refunded one thousand points for each full-credit course you successfully complete, and five hundred points for each half-credit course you successfully complete," Brett explains.

"The format is more or less a modified Dutch auction," Andy adds, "where the clearing price is determined by the lowest acceptable 'bid-ask' match. For example, if there are fifty open seats in the first round and sixty bids, clearly only fifty seats will trade. The price everyone pays for the fifty seats will be the lowest of the fifty highest bids. It gets a lot more complicated in the later rounds when all the seats for a class are taken and people begin to trade or drop classes. Not only do they submit bids for classes, but they enter 'asks' for the classes they no longer want or are trying to turn a profit on! It was a very complicated system to figure out."

"My bidding strategy wasn't complex. I reviewed the 'clearing' [successful] bids for similar courses in previous semesters, determined how important it was for me to take particular classes with particular professors, and placed my bids accordingly," Brett explains. "Since I rarely had the burning desire to take the most high-demand classes (those that cleared for three thousand or more points), getting the classes I wanted was a piece of cake."

Toby agrees: "While some students spend an inordinate amount of time trying to strategize and take advantage of point-arbitrage opportunities, I chose not to spend too much time trying to game the system. I spent my points on those classes that mattered most to me and found less personally important electives or time slots to fill in the remainder of my schedule."

"At Columbia, you really need to prioritize the classes you want most and put most of your points toward your top one or two picks," Anne adds.

Amy agrees: "At Haas, we each had one thousand points with which to bid on classes. We could divide that one thousand points any way we wanted. The key was to identify the classes and timeslots that were going to be popular by looking up last year's bidding data and talking to your classmates about what classes they were most interested in. At that point, you have to decide which popular class you want most, because if you end up splitting your points between two or three popular classes, the people who chose to focus all of their points on one class will outbid you."

Not everyone found the bidding process to be that competitive.

"I took finance classes at Kellogg," Kanna jokes, "so I used about one point for every class. I think I graduated with 25,345 points!"

Others pointed out that not all schools require you to bid on classes.

"At Tuck, you get all of the classes you want to take," Matt notes, "period. Any other system sucks—I mean you are the damn customer, right?"

Clearly, whether a school employs a bidding system for classes, and what that system is, becomes another point of distinction among schools. Some people love the bidding system. Others hate it. Whichever way you come out, just make sure you're adequately informed.

10

Getting Out of the Gate

"Put your shoulder to the wheel!"

— AESOP

STRATEGIES FOR SUCCESS IN THE FIRST YEAR

RETURNING TO SCHOOL after several years out in the business world can be pretty unnerving. After being out of the classroom for a few years (or more!), suddenly finding yourself back in an academic environment and surrounded by an amphitheater full of talented students competing for the same jobs and accolades can induce significant anxiety. Getting back in the swing of things may take a few weeks, but you'll get there. Be patient with yourself, give yourself plenty of time to get your work done, and prepare diligently for your classes, especially in the first few months of school. A few early successes can go a long way toward restoring your confidence in your academic abilities.

Determining Your Schedule

As a first-year business school student, at least for your first term or trimester, you will likely be enrolled in four core classes. Each of these classes will generally meet twice a week for two hours per session. At most schools, classes are scheduled four days a week, with the fifth day left open for groupwork, individual study, and extracurricular activities. You will generally have two classes per day on these four days, and as such, you will need to budget the necessary time to prepare for these classes the day before. By looking at the syllabi provided by your professors, you may be able to determine in advance the average amount of reading and prep work that each of your classes will require. While such estimates can be helpful in developing a workable schedule, it will probably take you at least a couple of weeks to get a good handle on how much prep time each class will generally demand.

At some point during the first week, try to rough out a schedule that includes your classes, your group meeting times, and your preliminary estimates for handling each course's reading assignments and/or case preparation. Sketch in time for meals, exercise, and school-related extracurricular activities. When you're done, take a step back and get a feel for what will be required of you in the coming year. While this allotment of your time will likely change somewhat, perhaps even dramatically, during the first few weeks, committing the totality of your weekly obligations to a written schedule will help reduce your anxiety about your ability to prepare adequately for classes, and will provide you with a readily accessible visual model to help keep you on track.

At this point, you may be saying to yourself, "Who do these people think I am, a high school student? I'm in professional school . . . I know how to budget my time to get assignments done."

If that is true, fantastic. But ask yourself an honest question: Is it really true?

"Every so often, you'll want to reassess how well business school is living up to your expectations. If there is a gap between what you're experiencing and what you had hoped to experience, then you'll need to readjust your day-to-day routine accordingly. Given the amount you're spending on business school, you do not want to be negligent about staying on course," Brett warns.

"There is simply not enough time to do everything, so leveraging one's time becomes critical," Andy adds. "Students in their first year can easily become overwhelmed. My advice is to stay centered and be willing to make some compromises with schedules. Never lose sight that your goal is to get the most out of the experience."

Dave agrees: "The first term is very hard. The adjustment back to school is difficult, so be sure to nail down your first term. Stay on top of things from the beginning, because this is not undergrad, where you may have been able to let some things slide for a while, and then made them up in the end. If you use that approach in business school, it will come back to haunt you."

Dave is right. Business school is not like college. You cannot blow off reading and classes for the entire semester and then cram for the exam the week before. You are expected to keep up on a daily basis, both by the professors and by the members of your work groups. Once classes begin, things move extremely quickly. Class material is covered rapidly; recruiting adds a whole other dimension and demand for your attention; and it is easy for the disorganized to fall behind. And once you're behind, it's not easy to catch up.

We mean no disrespect by suggesting that you write out a schedule for yourself. It is simply the time-tested, proven advice of those who have gone before you, that writing out a schedule and sticking to it—treating your business school obligations like a full-time job, and meeting daily expectations on deadline—is the best way to go.

If you map out a schedule, your typical day may look something like this:

TIME	COMMITMENT
7:00 A.M.–9:00 A.M.	Breakfast/review material for Class 1
9:00 A.M.–11:00 A.M.	Class 1
11:00 A.M.–1.00 P.M.	Lunch/errands/review material for Class 2

TIME	COMMITMENT
1:00 P.M.–3:00 P.M.	Class 2
3:00 P.M.–5:00 P.M.	Group meeting for a particular class
5:00 P.M.–6:30 P.M.	Work out
6:30 P.M.–7:30 P.M.	Dinner/relax
7:30 P.M.–11:00 P.M.	Read and prepare for Classes 3 & 4 (next day)
Spillover to weekend	Group meetings/read for Monday classes

"From my experience, the most demanding required work occurs from September to December of the first year, so be prepared to tough it out," Matt counsels. "I made a habit of looking ahead. I would start the following week's work on a Friday afternoon, and finish most of it at some point over the weekend. That way, I was able to do other things during the week like sports, activities, and helping my study-group members push through the areas of the material that I was already comfortable with. Don't sacrifice too much to stay on top of the work, but don't get behind, either. The worst feeling is starting to prep for a class late the night before that class, when all of your classmates are already in bed and not available for help."

TEACHING PHILOSOPHIES

The "Case" Method Versus the "Lecture" Method

The Case Method.

Business school classes are typically taught in one of two ways—either by straight lecture, or by using case studies to demonstrate the subject matter in context. In the case method, students review an actual business case study prior to class, and then proceed to break it down during class through questions and answers. In the lecture method, by contrast, professors deliver course material through straight lecture and notetaking, much like you remember from college. Some graduate programs employ one of these methods uniformly in all classes, while other schools leave the teaching method to the discretion of individual professors.

How to prepare a case study

To prepare a case study, read the case once through and just try to get the general gist of the business situation presented therein. Once you understand the scenario, review the questions posed by your professor at the end of the case, and then read the case a second time, making relevant notations in the margins. In the beginning, you may find that you need to read parts of the case several times in order to properly answer the questions. As with most things, though, you'll soon get the hang of it—and you'll improve with practice!

Keep a hard copy of your responses to the questions, and review any margin notes you've made on the case prior to the class discussion on it. Even a five-minute cursory review before class will prompt your recall memory and make the in-class discussion of the case much more meaningful to you. In classes taught using the case-study method, professors typically assign limited additional background reading to inform your understanding of the basic concepts raised or highlighted by the case. Doing this reading in advance of the class will, of course, provide you with a much richer understanding of the concepts at issue. If reading is assigned, it is worth doing.

The Lecture Method.

This is the teaching method you are likely to remember from college, where a professor stands in front of the lecture hall, and—hopefully in an engaging way—spoon-feeds the material to you. If your business school classes are taught in lecture format, you may find yourself *swamped* with reading. Lecture classes typically involve heavier reading loads than case-study classes, often because it takes much longer to explain concepts in the abstract than it does to illustrate them in the form of a concrete example from the business world.

It takes most students roughly the same amount of time to read material for a lecture as it does to properly analyze and prepare a case and do the necessary background reading, but most students harbor strong preferences for one teaching method over the other. Knowing how you prefer to learn may help you to choose courses that are better suited to those preferences—so after you have experienced each method at your school, put the question to yourself, and make your subsequent course selections according to your preference.

"I really enjoyed studying cases, but I feel that an education of basic principles makes for a better understanding of those cases," Alden explains.

Dave had the opposite reaction: "I prefer the case method. It offers everyone a chance to learn from each other with the professor acting as the moderator, injecting his expertise into the discussion when necessary."

"A combination approach that utilizes lecture with cases that highlight key ideas is the most comprehensive teaching approach," Toby notes. "I think that the case method works well for more qualitative courses like management, but can be disastrous for hard skills classes like accounting. Until you have learned the basic principles, a case experience that requires the application of those principles is ridiculous."

Cold-Calling

Whether a class is taught by the case method or by a straight lecture, many professors will engage in business school's version of "the Socratic method"—or what is commonly known as "cold-calling." A professor who employs strict "cold-calling" selects a student randomly and without warning from the seating chart to involuntarily respond to the professor's questions about that day's material. During the term, the professor will spread it around, but there is no guarantee that a student won't be called twice before another student is called once, so daily preparation becomes essential to avoid the embarrassment of being caught unprepared.

Cold-calling can be very intimidating, but if you prepare for class diligently on a daily basis, even if you didn't thoroughly understand the material, you should have some thoughts on how to respond to the professor's questions. Most professors do not cold-call with an intent to humiliate, so if you are truly stumbling, the professor will typically either guide you to the answer, or solicit help from your classmates.

The point behind cold-calling is to prepare you for the frequent real-world scenarios when you'll be put on the spot and forced to answer unanticipated questions about a project or subject matter you've been dealing with. By simulating these scenarios in class, the theory goes, you'll be more accustomed to dealing with surprise in a composed manner when it counts—in the business world.

Participation Counts

When you receive the syllabi for your first classes and examine the section of the syllabus that breaks down the components of the course grade, you will notice that most professors do consider the effectiveness of your class participation as a portion of your overall grade. Take this component seriously! While participation usually doesn't comprise more than 10 percent of your overall grade, in most classes, where exam and project grades are tightly clustered, that's the difference between a B and an A. And the difference between a B and an A in even a couple of classes in business school can have a dramatic impact on your overall class standing. Don't give up easy points by getting caught unprepared.

"When you have a concise and reasonable answer to a specific question, or if you have a new or unique idea or perspective to contribute to an open question, contribute!" Matt advises.

On the other hand: "There is a fine line between being an active participant in class, and being annoying. You shouldn't be shy or worried about saying something stupid, but you should also have respect for your classmates' intellect and give them a chance to express themselves," Alden explains.

"There are always a few individuals in a class who tend to dominate the conversation in every class period. These individuals are usually not viewed favorably by their peers," Toby observes.

"I think there is an unwritten rule against raising your hand more than twice in a given class," Andy concludes. "I think that's a good benchmark to follow."

SOME ADVICE ABOUT WORKING IN GROUPS

Many of your classes in business school will require a significant amount of work to be done in groups. This is done to simulate the working world, where any given project is typically handled by a project "team." Some professors will allow you to form your own groups. Others will assign you to working groups at random. Whatever the case, it is *essential* to your success and well-being in business school that you carry your share of the load for the group.

"Groupwork is essential to learning how to function in the business world. I am a product manager now and groupwork is basically the only way I do work."

—Amy

Be certain to show up on time and prepared for all group meetings. If you know you are going to be late, or if circumstances are going to force you to miss a group meeting, have the courtesy to inform your group members as far in advance as possible. Remember that when you miss a meeting or are late in arriving, it affects the schedules of every other member of your group as well—and it doesn't take many miscues to develop a reputation as an irresponsible group member who cannot be relied upon. Similarly, on occasions when your group divides up labor, take care to promptly and thoroughly complete the portions of assignments and other tasks you accepted responsibility for. Your group members don't want to hear that you are fighting with your significant other, battling your landlord, overwhelmed by recruiting demands, or struggling to complete assignments for other groups or other classes. Everyone in business school is under pressure, and has competing demands on their time. There is nothing more frustrating than having the group's progress stalled by a group member's failure to complete an assigned task on time. When you take responsibility for a task, *deliver.* It's as simple as that.

Now you might better understand why we told you to write out that schedule.

Finally, when working in a group, remember the basics of group dynamics. Listen to others' ideas, let others talk, contribute ideas of your own, and be willing to compromise. Business school is full of leaders, but not everyone can lead at the same time. Be willing to share responsibility equally for heading up tasks, and be certain to give credit where credit is due.

The consequences of being a bad groupmate, even in isolated

occurrences, can be significant. In schools where group members recommend each other's grades on projects to the professor, the consequences are often harsh and direct. Even if your school doesn't employ group grading, being an irresponsible group member can have significant indirect effects. Abdications of responsibility, whether intentional or inadvertent, will cause word to spread quickly, and as a result people will actively try to avoid working with you in the future. Conversely, developing a reputation as a reliable, hardworking, and productive group member can facilitate your membership in future groups of similarly exceptional students—which can have a direct effect on your grades in later classes. Your reputation is your currency in business school, and you'll carry your reputation with you from business school into the business world.

"You will learn by trial and error and through the blacklist whisperings in class, who is good to have as a group member and who is not," Dave suggests.

Take care to hold up your end of the bargain.

A second point to remember about groupwork is to engage and actively work *with* your groupmates. Chances are, each member of your group has had different work experiences and has developed different skill sets. "When you have the flexibility to choose your own groupmates, find people whose skills complement your own," Brett advises. "You no doubt have your own strengths that you'll want to share with the group, and you'll want partners who fill in the gaps, so that collectively, the group is well rounded."

This being so, do not simply assign the accounting part of a case analysis to the groupmate who has a CPA. If you have had little or no exposure to accounting prior to business school, work closely with your CPA groupmate, ask questions, encourage that groupmate to teach his skills to the others, and take the time to learn from him. During the course of a semester, each group member will likely have the opportunity to take the lead in teaching the others. The more such interaction you can engender in your groups, the more you stand to learn from the experience. In the pressure to get assignments completed and move on, don't lose sight of the fact that the learning process is paramount.

"Don't try to sit down and co-write something, and don't rewrite a teammate's work because you have a different writing style or would have said something a different way. Dividing and conquering usually works best with a project that requires a lot of writing. When it comes to problem sets and more empirical projects, it helps to sit down as a group and think it out together. Try to think out loud, because your thoughts can trigger other people's thoughts. It is a good idea to pick groupmates who have knowledge and thinking capacities that are complementary to yours. Some people will grasp certain concepts more quickly than others."

—Alden

A third and more practical recommendation about groupwork is to schedule meetings and meeting places as early as possible. Choice times in on-campus meeting spaces tend to get booked up early in the term, and you'll want to make sure that your group secures a convenient weekly meeting place with sufficient outlets for laptops and Ethernet connections. Furthermore, you'll want to get your weekly group meeting times into everyone's weekly calendars before their schedules get booked up with group meetings for other classes, extracurricular activities, and the like. The last thing you want is an eleven P.M. weekly meeting—so plan ahead!

Finally, if a professor permits you to form your own groups, act quickly to secure a good team. Consult the class rosters and check with your friends to find out who is in your classes, and strive to set up group commitments as early as possible. In your first term, few, if any, professors will allow you to self-select since no one really knows each other. In the second term or trimester and beyond, however, self-selection becomes common—so be on the ball to assure that you end up in a competent group. Since groupwork constitutes an important and significant part of your learning experience (and your overall grade in the class), the importance of ending up in a good group cannot be overstated.

"I would choose people who are willing to work hard, rather than one's friends," Anne concludes. "Having patience, setting an agenda for meetings, and dividing up responsibilities, are all useful strategies."

THE IMPORTANCE OF FIRST-TERM OR TRIMESTER GRADES

First-term grades in business school are critical to your summer internship applications if you intend to pursue positions with the large management-consulting or investment-banking firms. Since recruiting at these firms begins toward the end of your first term (or during the second trimester), if your school permits employers to ask about grades, your first set of grades provides one of the few ways for these firms to distinguish one student from another. Thus, getting off to a good start in business school is extremely important, because your first set of grades (along with the rest of your record, of course) gets you your summer internship—and the type of summer internship you get directly affects your effectiveness and success in second-year recruiting.

"I think the importance that people put on grades really depends on what industry you plan to enter," Amy explains. "Management-consulting and investment-banking firms care about grades, so if you want those jobs, you'll need to get the grades."

Other employers place less importance on grades and more importance on your background and overall experience.

"Grades were never a primary concern for me, because Yale downplayed their importance, and because I knew that I was not pursuing a career where my prospective employers would be looking at them," Alden notes.

"Don't worry about grades unless you want to do investment banking or consulting," David adds. "You're in business school to learn."

For this reason, an increasing number of business schools are enforcing grade-nondisclosure policies—policies which forbid on-campus recruiters from asking about your grades, and forbid you from sharing them with recruiters. This is another crucial point of distinction between schools—one that is worth taking into serious account when choosing a school. If you favor a learning environment where grades cannot be discussed or disclosed to employers, and where competition among students is significantly reduced as a result, you might want to look for schools that have implemented such policies. Call a school's career placement office to determine their official position on disclosure of grades.

What About Extracurricular Activities?

Beginning during orientation, or even before, you will be bombarded by clubs and associations vying for your interest and membership. Everyone from the Venture Capital Club to your business school's theatrical group will make a play for your attention.

Pace yourself!

Explore the various opportunities available to you, and then carefully pick the one or two activities that are of greatest interest to you and commit to them.

"Employ some strategic thinking in choosing what you become involved with," Matt advises. "Evaluate how an activity is going to help you achieve the overall goals you've set for business school."

"Involvement in extracurricular activities in business school is important for two reasons," Toby notes. "First, becoming involved in a preprofessional organization can provide you with an outlet to learn more about potential career opportunities. Second, involvement in extracurricular activities enables you to establish friendships and to network with people whom you might not otherwise have had the chance to meet. Finally, campus involvement, in general, demonstrates to prospective employers that you are well rounded and can effectively manage your time."

Don't become known as someone who pursues extracurricular activities as "résumé fillers"—eager to put the activity on your résumé while leaving responsibility for the heavy lifting to others—and don't overcommit to several activities but give none of them your full attention. As with your conduct in groupwork, your conduct in extracurricular activities will affect your overall reputation.

"I would choose one or two activities and focus on those," Amy suggests. "I tried to balance four during my first year and I felt overwhelmed."

Do your due diligence on the clubs and activities that interest you most, mindful that business school is only a two-year odyssey. It *is* true that some clubs require first-years to run for leadership positions as early as the end of the first term, and doing so does require you to have been active in the organization almost from the beginning. Accordingly, if you have an interest in becoming a leader in a particular club or activity, consider getting involved in that activity from the outset. But be selective, and *don't* overcommit.

11

The Unspoken Code of
Business School Etiquette

"Good manners will open doors
that the best education cannot."
— CLARENCE THOMAS

BUSINESS SCHOOL IS perhaps the quintessential "professional school" experience. Most people who attend business school have already spent several years out working in the business world, and have become acclimated to the social norms in that world. Returning to the classroom environment, however, imposes a new set of social norms—a canon of etiquette rules to govern your behavior and social interactions during business school. The two sets of social norms are occasionally divergent, and it is because of this divergence that people sometimes have trouble readjusting to the academic environment.

The code of business school etiquette is unspoken, and something you more or less have to figure out as you go along. The problem with this, of course, is that this learning process can be very stressful, deeply humiliating, and even permanently destructive, depending on which mistakes you make, and when and how you make them. Talk a little too much in class once or twice, and your classmates (*read:* future business contacts) will forgive you. Fail to deliver on an important responsibility to your work group even one time, however, and you might find yourself blacklisted for the rest of your life.

Consider this chapter, therefore, to be the first-ever "codification" of the rules of business school etiquette, as reported by your mentors. When these rules are followed, you end up with an environment where knowledge and understanding are shared freely among students; where in-class discussion is vigorous yet respectful; and where the pursuit of a business degree is made a truly pleasurable experience. When these rules aren't followed, you end up at a place where the educational experience degenerates into a dog-eat-dog world of competitiveness and one-upmanship.

Regardless of what school you attend, becoming familiar with these generally applicable rules will ease your assimilation back into the academic environment; will help to ensure that you remain in the good graces of the classmates who may well become your most important future business contacts; and, consequently, will assure that your business school experience will be as cooperative and collegial as possible.

THINGS YOU SHOULD DO

Respect the honor code.

Most undergraduate and graduate programs have honor codes. Though many schools will walk you through the honor code during a special meeting at the beginning of school, you should make sure to become familiar with your institution's honor code and system before you begin classes.

You might be wondering why a group of adults needs an honor code. After all, most likely you've worked in the real world for some time and think you know right from wrong. Right?

Unfortunately, in a loosely governed system, people cheat.

Honor codes exist to create a level of civility in the classroom and among the students, professors, and administration. Without an honor code and the imposition of consequences for violations, an environment of "everyone for himself" is likely to develop. If the rules stated in an honor code are followed and carried out, then an environment of trust and mutual respect is created among those involved.

In order for the honor code to work, all students must do their part. This includes the obligation to inform the disciplinary committee of any violations you witness or have learned about.

And why shouldn't you?

Aside from the fact that you should want to protect your academic environment from abuse, any benefit a violator derives from cheating may end up coming back to hurt *you*! If someone's cheating gets him a better grade on an exam or paper, it could influence the curve and affect the grade you earned fairly. If you're worried about alienating the cheater's friendship, you need not be. First, a friend who would cheat in business school is probably not a friend or business contact you're going to want to keep. Second, in nearly all cases, you can anonymously inform the proper authorities of violations of the honor code, in which case the individual(s) will never even know you were involved.

Many business schools have a system of publicly announcing all violations and all disciplinary-committee verdicts by way of a schoolwide e-mail. Specifics of the case are noted and the consequences of the honor code violations are made public, but no names are mentioned. This policy of making the details public and available to the rest of the student body helps to reinforce the honor code. It makes it clear to all the other students that the system works, and helps to deter future violations.

If students don't feel there is any consequence for cheating, then cheating will propagate. A successful honor code helps to eliminate misbehavior and develop a level playing field among all students.

Learn the honor code and your obligations under it. And remember that no matter how dire your circumstances may seem, there is never a good enough reason to cheat. If you're frustrated, or feeling desperate or overwhelmed, take a day off, ask your professor for some extra help, or go see the Dean of Students to request some relief. Extensions can be given. Leaves of absence can be granted. Short-term academic crises can almost always be worked out.

Don't ever lose sight of the fact that if you cheat even once and get caught, you'll carry that mark around with you for a lifetime.

Always come to class prepared.

Showing up completely unprepared for a class discussion is disrespectful to the professor and to your classmates—particularly in case-based teaching environments where your participation is counted on to help teach others. There does also seem to be some cosmic law that says when you come to class ill-prepared, that's the class where you'll get cold-called.

If a professor does catch you on an off-day, don't waste the class's time trying to B.S. your way through an answer. If you simply admit to being unprepared and offer a quick apology, the professor will likely move on to someone else. But don't mistake the professor's speedy redirection as getting out of such a predicament unscathed. Most professors make a note of such incidents, and the participation component of your grade will likely suffer as a result.

Remember, though, that you're not in business school for the grades. You're there to learn, and the fact is you're not likely to get much out of a class if you can't follow the discussion. It's especially difficult to take anything from a case analysis if you haven't even read the case.

Finally, remember that business school is *professional* school.

You're not in college anymore. In college, when you arrived in class unprepared and got busted for it, your classmates generally laughed with you rather than *at* you. In business school, in addition to hurting your grade, arriving at a class unprepared can damage your reputation, because it says something about how seriously you take the experience.

Class clowns don't make good work-group members—and don't make good business contacts, either. Remember that.

Share your class notes.

Business schools try to foster an environment based on teamwork. On any given day, and for a variety of valid reasons (particularly during recruiting season), people are going to miss class and come looking to photocopy your lecture notes or case analyses.

Let them.

Helping out your classmates in times of need builds bridges. People remember the favors you do for them. The day will come when you need a favor returned. Building up some "favor equity" in your classmates is never a bad thing.

Save tangential questions or comments for after class or during office hours.

If you find yourself interested in a topic that diverges from the main class discussion, hold your question until after class or for office hours. Professors have their classes well planned and generally need all the time allotted in order to teach the principles of the course and to keep the class's progress through the material on track.

Your classmates will not appreciate your monopolizing class time with a divergent discussion that only you find interesting—

and will particularly resent any politically charged diatribe you might make against a company or its conduct. Remember that your class is composed of all parts of the political spectrum. You risk alienating many of your classmates by taking the class on a journey through your knee-jerk political reactions to the various scenarios that come up. Unless the professor *specifically* solicits feedback of a political nature, keep your political views under your hat.

Raise your hand—and do not speak out of turn.

You've been hearing this rule since first grade, but you'd be amazed at how many people continue to violate it. Chances are, during your business school career, you will experience a range in levels of class formality. Some professors will establish complete authority and will control student commentary through cold-calling. Other professors will establish a less formal environment by allowing and encouraging active discussion among students.

While the latter environment is plainly more comfortable for most students, it is also more fraught with perils to the unwary. Make a mental note to speak only when you feel you have something significant to contribute to the dialogue, and when you do, wait to be recognized and to be given the floor. While the professor is encouraging widespread class participation he or she will want to control who contributes, and how often. It's not likely a professor will call on you more than twice during a class, so pick your spots. Professors want everyone to contribute, for a diversity of opinions and perspectives.

Every class has its blowhard who feels his opinion matters more than everyone else's: the person who always has to get in the last word . . . the person who always has his hand in the air . . . the person who tells his classmates they are wrong in open lecture; the person who laughs at other people's comments; the person who is so busy coming up with the next thing *he* wants to say that he fails to listen to what others in the class are saying.

Don't be that person.

Ask your classmates questions (after class).

Your classmates are a great source of knowledge and advice. Prior to business school, you all will have had unique business experiences and gained varied skills and knowledge. If you find yourself in a corporate finance class after working in marketing prior to school, you will likely have a steeper learning curve than your fellow classmate who spent four years in investment banking. Rather than viewing your classmate as fierce competition, regard him or her as a source of knowledge and aid!

Don't be concerned about appearing stupid in front of a classmate by asking for help from them. He or she may have extensive knowledge in corporate finance but may know nothing about taking a new consumer product from preproduction to market. Remember that everyone comes to business school with different skill sets, and if you ask someone a question about his specialty, he may feel more comfortable coming to *you* in another class. It's also a psychological truism that asking other people for their help and advice makes them feel good about themselves, which, in turn, will make them like you more.

Don't go through business school in a vacuum, and don't just rely on the people in your work group or study group. There is a whole world of experience out there in your class! Take advantage of all the bright minds around you. Business schools recognize the value of their students' experiences and knowledge and encourage students to communicate and exchange information among one another.

Respect your professor's rules of engagement.

No matter how absurd your professor's rules may seem, always be aware of and abide by them. Some professors will have stringent rules about the operation of their classes, while others may not specifically address the subject, leaving fairness and appropriate conduct up to the rules of the honor code.

Generally, professors will review their rules during the first class meeting; these rules are also likely to be published in the professor's course packet. Rules may include things like assigned seating, guidelines for getting extensions, policies on tardiness and absenteeism, and more.

Though some rules may appear extreme, your professor has instituted them for a reason. If a rule seems particularly unfair or unreasonable, raise the issue *privately* with the professor during office hours.

Respect your classmates.

Your classmates will likely hail from all over the world, speak different languages, come from different cultures, and, as such, may have very different religious, cultural, or familial demands on them outside the school environment. Be sensitive to these and other differences between you and your classmates.

In many situations these differences can really help your group. Often, several different perspectives or approaches to the same problem will ultimately help your group come to a more complete solution. Occasionally, however, these differences can also become a source of conflict.

Students who speak English as a second language, for instance, may not be the strongest writers, may take longer to get their point across, or may speak up less frequently in meetings because they are worried about their English skills. Be sure to give these individuals plenty of opportunity to speak in group meetings, and be patient with their explanations. You may also find that a group-mate seems to perpetually be late to meetings. Before you go off half-cocked, investigate whether a cultural difference is the explanation. In some cultures, arriving ten or fifteen minutes late for meetings is considered normal, and as such, it is possible the person may not be aware that they are delaying the start of the meeting. A simple explanation of the group's expectations should suffice to cure the problem.

Lastly, you should try to be respectful of each groupmate's outside pressures and obligations. If a group member observes a holy day, you'll need to work your meetings around it. Some group members may be involved in a long-distance relationship, or may be married with children. While business school responsibilities are important, they are not more important than a sick child. Be respectful of your groupmates' lives outside of school and try to be flexible when scheduling meetings or assigning work.

Talk to your professors.

If you went to a large undergraduate university with large classes, this concept may be new to you. During college you may have found it nearly impossible even to schedule time with the teaching assistants, let alone the actual professor. Business school is much different. In most cases, professors are excited about teaching young, business-minded students, and are eager to meet with you outside of class. Don't miss out on this incredible opportunity!

You should get to know your professors for several reasons. Obviously, these individuals have a wealth of knowledge and they can help clarify questions you may have from lecture or readings. Another reason, though, is that many of your professors act as consultants or may have worked in business before becoming professors, and therefore are likely to have a lot of contacts in the business world. Just as your fellow classmates can be useful in generating a network, so can your professors.

Don't hesitate to establish professional relationships with your professors to help facilitate these sorts of conversations.

THINGS YOU SHOULDN'T DO

Don't overcommit.

Although we've mentioned this before, it is worth reiterating here. The first-year workload, responsibilities to your groupmates, and recruiting, will consume an inordinate amount of your time each week. Extracurricular clubs can also be very time-consuming. Exactly *how* time-consuming will depend upon your level of leadership within the organization, but even rank-and-file members will have meetings once a week, or once every two weeks. If you are involved in five or six clubs or groups, the hours can add up quickly.

You will likely find yourself being recruited by at least a dozen different organizations. Do not be flattered or coerced into joining a club that you are not fully committed to. Early in your first year, it is easy to fall victim to the solicitations of some clubs you ordinarily wouldn't chose to devote your time to. Be patient and research each club carefully before joining.

You may find yourself tempted to join various clubs and organizations to help build up your résumé. While employers do look for interesting extracurricular activities, recruiters are more interested in your roles *within* those organizations, what you contribute to them, and what you get out of them, rather than the *number* of clubs you belong to. You are better off having a more significant role within two or three organizations than simply being a member of five or six.

Your classmates, and particularly second-year students, will be on the lookout for people who overcommit to clubs for perceived résumé value. Do not remain a member of a club if you don't plan to make a significant contribution to it. We've all known people who promise things and fail to deliver, and those people are never thought of very highly.

Do not surf the 'Net or fiddle with a Blackberry during class.

As the world becomes more "wired," so do business schools. Not only do most study rooms have access to the school network and the Internet, so will many of your classrooms. Furthermore, wireless e-mail and Internet now makes it possible to stay connected virtually 24/7. Having the *ability* to connect to the network or the Internet, however, *does not* mean you should do so during class.

During the first day of classes, many professors will state their policy regarding connecting to the network during class time. Many will prohibit students from plugging in and will watch for violators. Conversely, others may *require* you to be connected to the network during class in order to have the capacity to view various class materials or to visit the websites or filings of companies under discussion.

If your class is not using the Internet to facilitate discussion, go offline, and shut down your cell phone and your Blackberry. You are paying top dollar to get an education. During the hours you are in class, those classes should be your highest priority. There is no greater exhibition of arrogance than allowing your cell phone to ring, or responding to e-mails during a lecture— and nothing will raise the ire of your classmates more quickly.

Never let your group down.

This may be the most important rule of etiquette of all. You will find that scheduling group meetings can be an enormous challenge. Finding mutual open time across four or five schedules can be unbelievably difficult. So the first rule of group work is: *Never* skip a scheduled meeting—and move heaven and earth to avoid being late. Do not make your group members wait for you.

It is all about respect for others. Your groupmates are busy, too. Don't put your needs ahead of theirs. If a conflict arises in your schedule that is *completely* unavoidable, you should contact your groupmates *immediately* to let them know about the conflict and why you will not be able to make the meeting. At this point, your group will decide whether they can carry on without you or whether it is necessary to reschedule. If your group keeps the scheduled meeting time, you will still need to get your part of the work to the rest of your group prior to the meeting. While everyone will have a conflict now and then (and you should be understanding of these sorts of conflicts, if they are uncommon), do not look to your groupmates again and again to let you out of meetings and responsibilities.

Second, if you're going to be late to a meeting, you should call or e-mail one or all of your groupmates. Sometimes being late is unavoidable. A professor might keep you late, or a phone call with a potential employer may run over. Again, just don't make it a habit.

A third hard-and-fast rule for group work is to always have your work for the group done on time. At the end of each meeting you and your group are likely to determine who is responsible for what material and when it is due to be shared with the group. Do not be late with your contribution. If you know at the time assignments are dispersed within the group that you won't have time to complete your responsibilities by the agreed-upon due date, be honest with your groupmates *up front.* If you speak up in advance, the group can make adjustments.

The absolute worst thing you can do is promise something and not deliver. In many cases, the next part of the project will rely on your piece being completed. Slowing down the group in this way, even once, is a *big* no-no.

The consequences of violating any of these rules can be long-lasting. The most damaging outcome of being a bad groupmate is getting "blacklisted." Once you are blacklisted, your name will get passed among your classmates as someone to avoid putting in a group. When you offend or let down your group, your group-mates will get frustrated and they *will* tell others. As a result, you will find it harder and harder to find groupmates.

Being a poor groupmate can also cost you friendships. The following tale is illustrative.

> "We had one groupmate who missed a few meetings and was late with a couple of assignments because he was more fo-cused on his efforts to succeed in the recruiting process. The rest of the group became quite frustrated and aggravated by his lack of attention and communication. I mean, we were all recruiting, too! Finally we decided to make this person aware of the group's feelings. He reacted defensively, became quite angry that we weren't more understanding of his efforts to find employment, and broke off his friendships with all of us. As a result, he received poor peer-evaluation grades from everyone in the group, and was the only member of our group not to get an A on the group project—because the professor took our peer-evaluation grades and comments seriously."
>
> —a mentor

Don't arrive late to class.

Arriving late to class is rude and disrespectful to your professor and to your classmates. Repeated tardiness may lead to your professor pulling you aside and reprimanding you, or even dropping your grade.

If you have to arrive late to class, slip in quietly, and disturb the class as little as possible. Take an empty seat in the back and excuse and explain your tardiness to your professor *after* class so that he or she understands that you had a reasonable explanation for coming late.

Respect *matters* in the business world, and showing up to class prepared and on time is all about demonstrating respect.

Display humility, not arrogance.

When you make a comment in class or during a conversation with classmates, avoid coming across as a know-it-all. Professors and fellow classmates dislike it equally. Steer clear from making too many references to your own personal experiences, or making comments such as, "When I was at [*insert big-name company here*] we never used that method of analysis." While you may feel that your experiences are particularly applicable to a given subject, before you open your mouth, entertain the possibility that many of your classmates may have had relevant experiences as well. If you all told the stories of your "relevant" experiences, the professor would never get to complete the lecture and your classmates would be bored to tears.

If you are genuinely questioning a point your professor has made, try presenting your concern in the context of a question. You can make the above point the same way, for example, by raising your hand and stating: "I am more familiar with a different method of analysis X. Could you discuss the differences between the two?" In this manner you are able to make the same point without appearing arrogant or antagonistic.

The same rule applies in your interactions with your fellow

students. Do not try to impress your classmates with stories of grandeur from your life before business school. Rather than being blown away by your business acumen, more likely, other students will make a mental note to avoid future conversations with you.

In general, it is best to err on the side of humility. You can prove your superior intelligence to your professors by performing well on exams and/or papers. Your friends will appreciate and enjoy your company more for your character and personality than for your "superior" business acumen.

Don't attempt to show up classmates during lecture.

Building on the previous rule, do not attempt to show up your classmates during lecture. Though you may know that a comment made by a classmate is inaccurate, or you may know the answer to a question he or she has posed to the professor, do not try to correct or answer his or her question out of turn. It is not your job to do so, and doing so might unnecessarily embarrass your classmate.

Professors do not appreciate students trying to outshine their classmates. In the largely cooperative and collegial business-school learning environment, such tactics are seen as cruel and unnecessary—and, if done repeatedly, may discourage other students from contributing to class discussions. While you may think others will be impressed by your superior intelligence, you are really just alienating classmates and damaging your professor's image of you.

Do not have side conversations in class.

Though we advocate asking fellow classmates for help, do not engage in conversation during class. It is virtually impossible to have a side conversation that goes completely unnoticed. At a bare minimum you will distract the people around you. Worse yet, your professor could become irritated by your rude and dis-respectful chat and publicly ask you to cease the conversation.

Again, it's a matter of respect.

If you feel that you need clarification on a point, or that a professor has glossed over something, raise your hand and ask your professor to clarify it. You may actually be helping others who are also unclear on the subject. If you are still unclear, wait until after class to have a conversation about it.

Avoid name-dropping.

Ah, yes—the *biggie.*

Perhaps the most obvious and most common faux pas of busi-ness school is the not-so-artful act of name-dropping. Undoubt-edly you will hear a number of classmates, especially early in your first year, talking about knowing so-and-so, the CEO of some For-tune 500 corporation, or some other well-known executive whom they claim to have worked closely with, to know personally, or to have recently spoken with.

The only reason people name-drop is because they're insecure about their own accomplishments and abilities, and feel they need to do something in order to impress or get a leg up on their fellow classmates.

The corollary rule is simply not to brag about anything. Don't talk to your classmates about your undergraduate GPA, your GMAT score, or the salary you've just been offered by company X. All your classmates were accepted to your school for a reason; rather than trying to "one-up" them, try learning something from them.

No one likes name-droppers.

No one.

Don't be one of them.

12

How to Succeed in the First-Year Summer Recruiting Process

> "The crowning fortune of a man
> is to be born to some pursuit which finds him
> happiness and employment..."
> — EMERSON

JUST AS YOU begin to get settled into your classes, and probably before you become comfortable with your routine, the barrage of e-mails and notices about summer internships will begin. Initially these notifications will inform you about résumé-writing workshops; seminars about how to determine career objectives; and opportunities to take personality tests to match you with complementary job opportunities. These seminars are optional, but usually interesting, and, in many cases, even pretty helpful.

The résumé-writing seminar and materials can be especially helpful in your preparation of a properly targeted résumé for your school's all-important Résumé Book. In schools that compile one, a Résumé Book is a consolidation of all students' résumés, which is published and sold to large corporations. These companies buy a business school's Résumé Book, review the résumés in it, and contact the students they deem attractive. Entire books have been written on the subject of crafting a winning résumé, so we won't be going back over that here. Instead, we'll simply underscore the importance of two primary points to remember.

First, be sure that your résumé is well crafted, targeted, and flawless. Remember, to potential employers, your résumé is your calling-card. How your information is presented, what you choose to include, how carefully it is targeted, and how well it is written—all make a significant impression. While your résumé alone won't win you a job offer, a poorly crafted résumé, thrown together at the last minute, may guarantee you won't have a chance to make a second impression. Secondly, be sure that you finalize and submit your résumé to your school's career management office well in advance of the deadline for Résumé Book submissions. Forgoing an opportunity to be included in your school's Résumé Book is unwise. You never know who might come a-callin'!

Your first task as you enter the first-year recruiting process is to hearken back to the analysis you did prior to applying to business school, recall exactly why it is you are there, and what it is you hope to take out of the experience. The beginning of the first-year recruiting process is an important time to take your bearings because it is precisely where a number of people lose their way.

"Focus on what it is that you want to do," Amy suggests. "It is all too easy to get competitive and apply for the hottest, most selective positions, whether you want those jobs or not. Doing that will only divert your time and attention away from the job you'd really like to have, as opposed to the job you think you want to get. Don't lose sight of the difference between the two."

The first-year summer also provides an opportunity to explore new possibilities, since most students reenter the recruiting pool during the second year anyway.

"Be flexible," Alden notes. "Remain open-minded to possibilities you hadn't thought of before. Apply to jobs in a variety of locations, and use the summer as a chance to test out something you're not sure you'll like, or as a chance to get some experience that will be useful in, but is peripheral to, your intended career path."

Organization is the key to the summer internship application process. You will likely be applying to a number of companies—and for different positions. In order to keep track of deadlines, application requirements, contact information, and the like, you may find it helpful to create a database to manage this information. Include columns for application deadlines, contact information, interview dates and times, communications you have with each company, what you have submitted to each company (and when you submitted it), and whatever else you think will help you manage the process more effectively.

You might also find it helpful to create a paper filing system, with a physical folder for each company to which you are applying. Keep all the information and research you collect on each firm, and a copy of everything you send to each firm, in that firm's file. The application process generates *a lot* of paperwork, and requires you to be able to structure and organize a lot of information. You cannot be too diligent in this regard.

Once you've set up your database, monitor it regularly and keep it current. Use your database to help you stay on top of deadlines, and be sure to submit all application materials several days ahead of any deadline. Submissions received at the deadline, even if they are perfect, can leave recruiters with the impression that your application was an afterthought, or that you're disorganized or a procrastinator—neither of which is a sought-after attribute in managers and business leaders.

Get off on the right foot with a company by filing your application materials in a timely fashion. A side benefit of doing so is that recruiters have been known to peek at early files to "see how the pool is shaping up." If you are an attractive candidate and your materials are in, you may benefit from being more readily identified during one of these early looks than you would be in among a pile of submissions that all arrive at the deadline.

THE "FORMAL" SUMMER INTERNSHIP APPLICATION PROCESS

We will use the term "formal recruiting" to describe the recruiting process that is managed by your school's career management office. Companies participating in this process are generally Fortune 1000 companies and other large organizations that routinely hire graduates of your school, and may also be large financial supporters of the school. Because of this, the career management office will manage and organize most recruiting events and the interviewing process for these companies.

Recruiting Events

Recruiting begins in earnest in late October with the first arrivals of what will ultimately become a barrage of potential employers visiting campus. A business school "recruiting event" can generally be defined as a company presentation, followed by an hour or so of cocktails, appetizers, and mingling. There are several key things to know about these events. First, if you are even *remotely* interested in a company putting on a recruiting event, be sure to show up, stay at least long enough to have one or two targeted conversations, and sign in. Companies usually have sign-in sheets at these events which they later use to cross-check and verify the level of interest of candidates at a particular school. An unexplained absence from the on-campus recruiting event of a company you've applied to indicates your interest in the company is lukewarm at best, and often will exclude you from further interviewing. So show up and sign in, even if you cannot stay for the entire event. If you *must* miss the on-campus recruiting event of a company to which you've applied, it is generally a good idea to call the hiring partner or recruiting coordinator at the firm, reaffirm your interest, and excuse your absence in advance.

At the event itself, hang around for the cocktail hour if at all possible. Introduce yourself to the company's representatives (typically, alumni of your school, or at least other M.B.A.s). Ask pertinent questions about the company; but stay away from the simple questions like, "How large is the company?" or, "Where are the company's major offices?"—which reflect the fact that you haven't done your homework. Your goal is to make a favorable impression, distinguishing you in the minds of the people you talk to. Before ending a conversation with an alumnus or other company representative, collect a business card so you have someone to contact with any questions; this also says to the individual, *I enjoyed our conversation and you've piqued my interest enough to want to follow up.*

"It's very important to attend these sorts of information sessions so that you get a chance to meet representatives from each of the firms and get a feel for the different corporate cultures," Toby advises. "Don't worry so much about getting face time with the human-resources representatives that come to campus. Use the mingling opportunities as a means to get a feel for the [company], and answers to the substantive questions you have. Ask the same question of multiple people and compare their answers!"

"Always dress appropriately for these events, and don't spend too much time socializing with your classmates or consuming the free refreshments. You should make it a point to make direct personal contact with at least one company representative at each presentation. I would also have one really good question prepared," Andy notes.

Invitation-Only Events

There will be some on-campus recruiting events that are "invitation-only." Invitations to these events are extended by the company to individuals identified and targeted by their résumés in the Résumé Book, or by referral from a reliable source known to the company. These invitation-only events are held after the open cocktail events, and constitute the second round of a company's recruiting. At these events, there will likely be another presentation, and you will again be surrounded by company representatives—but the ratio of company representatives to recruits will be significantly lower, and the attention focused on you by these representatives will be more direct.

"Be sure to come prepared to these events," Toby adds. "You'll want to be familiar with all of the readily available information on a company's website, and any other information about the company that you can obtain, in case it comes up in discussion."

Toward the end of the first round of recruiting events, cover-letter and résumé submissions are due for candidates seeking spots on major corporations' closed-interview lists. At most schools, this process begins around the beginning of December.

The Basics of Interviewing

In your first year, most interviews will begin as soon as you return from winter break. In order to hit the ground running when you get back, it is best to do your interview preparation before you leave for the holidays.

You should *never* walk into an interview without having done some advance research about the company. In addition to providing companies with an opportunity to learn more about you, the interview also gives companies an opportunity to gauge your level of interest in *them*. If you appear to know little or nothing about the company you are interviewing with, the interviewer will likely conclude that you are minimally interested in his company. Even if the interviewer decides that you are well qualified for the position, a perceived lack of interest is often enough to seal a rejection.

Enter all interviews with a few questions prepared ahead of time. Asking insightful questions during an interview is seen as an expression of genuine interest in the company and will convey the sincerity of your pursuit of employment there. More importantly, the interview is an opportunity to actually get answers to your more specific questions about the position you are seeking and what it would be like to work there. Do some due diligence in coming up with your questions, and avoid asking those that could easily be answered by spending five minutes on the company website. Asking "canned" questions about readily available statistics, numbers, and office locations just makes you look lazy and uninformed.

If you are not interested enough in a company to do some serious prep work for the interview, you should not be taking the interview slot away from another candidate. It's as simple as that.

The Opening Round: "Closed-List" versus "Open-List" Interviews

Whether your school offers "closed-list" interviews, "open-list" interviews, or a combination of both, largely depends on how well respected your school is, and how anxious a company is to come to campus to interview students at your school. At lesser-ranked schools, companies might not come to campus at all were they not allowed to "cherry-pick" the best students for closed-list interviews.

So, what is all this lingo? you ask.

"Closed-list" interviews are offered by the company directly to individual students after the company's review of cover letters and résumés, or the submissions in your school's Résumé Book. In essence, these interviews represent a company's "top picks" from your school. Students who do not get a closed-list interview, however, can usually still sign up for an interview on a company's "open" list.

What's the big deal, then?

First, your school may impose a "bidding system" or quota

limiting the number of open interviews you can take. At most schools, the number of closed interviews you earn does not affect this quota. Second, open-interview candidates often face an uphill battle. Since the company has already reviewed the Résumé Book, and hand-selected the candidates it wants to see for the closed-list interviews, in all likelihood these candidates were passed up during their initial screening process.

With this in mind, you may now be wondering why a company even bothers to take open interviews.

Open lists are the career management center's way of providing equal opportunity to all students. In many cases, schools require companies to provide a certain number of open list interview slots as a condition of their participation in that school's on-campus recruiting events. If the school and its students are well respected by the company, it will concede to this requirement. If not, the company may pull out of the campus. All of that notwithstanding, interviews still animate candidates in a way that cover letters and résumés cannot, and as such, there are always open-list candidates not initially selected for a closed-list interview who end up getting hired by a particular company. Though closed-list candidates definitely have the upper hand, it is not uncommon for open-list candidates to break through into the second round of interviews where the playing field is level again.

Later Rounds

First-round interviews are typically followed by a second round, and in some cases, third and even fourth rounds. Second-round interviews are offered to the most promising candidates from the first round at whom the recruiter wants a closer look. For many companies, second-round interviews involve "fly-backs" to the company's offices, though some may occur on campus either the same day or the day following the first-round interviews. If you are invited on a fly-back interview at the company's offices, you will often spend all morning, afternoon, or possibly even the entire day interviewing with a number of employees. These interviews are typically designed to determine your "fit" with the company's culture, or to allow more senior decision-makers at the company to weigh in on your candidacy.

THE THREE TYPES OF RECRUITING INTERVIEWS

There are three major categories of interviews: résumé interviews, "fit" interviews, and "case" interviews. These three categories are not mutually exclusive—you may get a few questions of each type, or questions of only one type in any given interview, depending on the industry, the round, and the experience and mood of the interviewer.

Résumé interviews are used by most companies for at least part of the interview—particularly in the initial rounds, where recruiters are looking for a better picture of who you are, which they can most easily get by asking you to elaborate on your experiences. "Fit" interviews are typically used in the second and later rounds, and focus more on your personality and probe topics to determine whether you will fit in well at the firm. Although "fit" interviews frequently broach some of the same "experiential" subjects as those discussed in résumé interviews, "fit" interviews tend to be more conversational and less formal. "Case" interviews, which dominate in the consulting and investment-banking fields, are exactly the opposite. Intellectually rigorous, these interviews ask you to respond extemporaneously to a hypothetical business scenario or problem posed by the interviewer—using the best analytical skills you can muster, given the facts you have. In "case" interviews, the interviewers are especially interested in how you respond to the pressure of the situation, and how you reason through the question to a conclusion.

We discuss each method of interviewing, and provide tips and advice for each type, below.

Résumé Interviews

Not surprisingly, perhaps, résumé interviews focus on your background, credentials, and work experience, and interviewers using this methodology are likely to seek elaboration from you about particular experiences or issues raised by your résumé. Common topics raised in these interviews include situations in which you have been required to demonstrate particular leadership, organizational, communication, and problem-solving skills, or where you have demonstrated your ability to take initiative and work within a team.

Though it may seem obvious to point out, your first step in preparing for a résumé interview is to master your résumé. Know it cold, and be prepared to discuss and defend anything that appears on it. Often, discussions in résumé interviews orbit around what you would consider to be your more "minor" activities and interests—so be sure you are not overreaching: Don't claim to be fluent in Spanish unless you are ready to read and speak it in an interview, and don't claim to be an expert fly-fisherman if you aren't ready to discuss your fly-tying skills, favorite spots, and most reliable strategies with your interviewer. Many a student has been derailed in an interview by being caught exaggerating on a résumé.

When facing questions about your experience, formulate your answers using the "STAR" method (*situation, task, action, result*). Begin your discussion by describing the *situation* and the *task* that confronted you. Next, explain the *actions* you took, step by step, to address the situation or task. Finally, discuss the *results* of your actions—what was accomplished, not just by you, but for the organization as a whole, as well as what skills you gained, and what you learned from the experience. Think about the STAR steps for each topic on your résumé so you'll have something to say about anything on your résumé if you are asked about it. Don't overrehearse your answers so much that your responses seem "canned," but take the time to think about each item highlighted on your résumé and how you can use it to put your best foot forward if you are called upon to discuss it in an interview.

Ultimately, you want your responses to be concise and focused on your performance and accomplishments, and how these accomplishments affected the "big picture" at your company. Stay away from long-winded explanations or more general discussions about your company's achievements—interviewers are trying to discern *your* abilities and potential in a very short period of time. Don't waste valuable interview time on a drawn-out story about how the CEO of your former company selected a new parts supplier that ultimately changed the way your company, and its entire industry, did business *unless* you played a critical role in bringing about that change.

In thinking through STAR responses for your résumé items, focus on the following key skills that firms will be most interested in seeing you demonstrate. These skills are listed below, followed by a number of *actual* interview questions experienced by the mentors and used to draw out information about each of these skills.

General Attributes

- What was the greatest challenge you've had to face in your life so far?
- What do you consider to be your most important accomplishment?
- What is the hardest you have ever had to work at something?
- What has been your most significant disappointment to date?
- What was your most humbling experience?

- What is your biggest weakness?
- What is the area of your life in which you feel you most need to improve?
- What has been your most valuable learning experience to date?

Leadership Skills

- Give me an example of a situation where you demonstrated leadership.
- What was the greatest challenge that you were able to overcome using leadership?
- Tell me about a time when you set the direction for a group.
- What do you think are the most valuable attributes a leader can have?
- How would you handle yourself if you were called upon to lead someone who neither liked you nor respected you?
- What historical or business leader do you most admire, and why?

Organizational Skills

- Give me an example in which you were able to successfully manage multiple projects at one time.
- What strategies do you use to balance your projects?
- You are working on a significant project for a partner that is due in forty-eight hours. While you were out of your office, another partner has dropped off a piece of a project that must be completed in the same forty-eight-hour period. How would you handle this?
- Provide an example of how you have effectively employed multitasking in your life.

Communication/Interpersonal Skills
- Tell me about a time when you had to make an unpopular decision and get others to commit to it.
- Give me an example of a difficult situation where you were able to convince your colleagues of your recommendations on a course of action, and how you accomplished this.
- Give an example of how you have dealt with difficult personalities in the workplace.
- Give me an example of a difficult management situation you faced and how you were able to motivate your team to accomplish your goals.

Analytical/Problem-Solving Skills
- Give me an example of a project in which you had to collect data and make recommendations.
- Tell me about a project that challenged your analytical skills.

Initiative/Motivation
- How have you motivated other people over whom you had no authority? How did you achieve results, and what results did you achieve?
- Tell me about your last job: What did you personally do that changed how the company did business or otherwise made a difference?

Teamwork
- How would you handle working under a leader you didn't respect?
- What were the attributes you brought to the last team you worked on?
- What are the skills you respect most in team members?

- How would you handle a situation where you were forced to work on a team with a co-worker who didn't like you?

As you may have already discerned from looking over these questions, the questions themselves are not especially complicated. After all, all they do is ask you to reflect and comment on the experiences you've had in your own life! What these questions do require, however, is some advance thought, reflection, and preparation.

There is no reason you should ever get caught off-guard by a résumé question.

"Fit" Interviews

"Fit" interviews generally occur in the second and third rounds of interviewing and focus on you as a person. These interviews feel more relaxed because interviewers will engage you in more-casual conversation in an effort to explore your personality and your work experience. You may find yourself discussing topics as diverse as the state of the economy and the state of your golf game. Being granted a "fit" interview is generally a good sign, as these interviews are typically used by firms to screen out people whose credentials (and possibly even performance in a prior résumé interview) met company requirements, but whose personalities make them incompatible with the firm's culture or work environment.

"Case" Interviews

The typical "case" interview begins with a brief exchange of pleasantries and perhaps a brief review of a point or two of interest from your résumé. After that, you will be asked to spend the balance of the interview crunching numbers to try and "crack" a hypothetical case posed by the interviewer.

"Huh?" you ask.

Take it easy. It's not as scary as it sounds, but we're not going to sugar-coat it, either—"case" interviewing can be unnerving, and is the place where most business school students get tripped up.

Typically the interviewer will begin by explaining that you are about to be given a hypothetical case. At this point, you should bring out pen and paper and take notes as the interviewer describes a business situation, followed by a question or series of questions. Your job, when the interviewer is finished speaking, is to come up with the most appropriate or fitting answer to the question(s) posed.

When the interviewer has finished presenting the initial case scenario and related questions, ask for some time to gather your thoughts. Though the silence may feel uncomfortable, don't feel compelled to fill the silence with silly banter. Collect yourself and analyze the issues as if the interviewer weren't even in the room. Do not expect to have an answer right away. In most cases, the information provided at the onset is insufficient to properly answer the question(s) and, as such, you will need to probe the interviewer for more information. Take a few minutes to prepare your thoughts and write down a few questions that solicit from the interviewer whatever follow-up information you feel you'd need to have to complete the analysis properly.

As you move forward with your analysis, speak out loud, and write your thoughts and analysis down. *Explain your thought process to the interviewer*, as well as the methods of analysis you are using, why you have chosen a particular line of analysis, and why you are drawing the conclusions you are. Do any calculations in writing, as it is not uncommon to find the interviewer looking closely at your notes and following your analysis. In many cases, your interviewer will collect any written work you have done, both to examine your analysis, and to ensure that you won't share your work with your classmates who may be interviewing later. Do not worry about getting to the "right" answer. In some cases, there isn't even a "right" answer. "Case" interviews are used, for the most part, to get a close-up, on-the-spot view of a candidate's analytical skills and his or her ability to think quickly under pressure.

When you feel you have a good answer to the question(s) posed by the interviewer, quickly review your analysis for any gaping holes, facts you've overlooked, other methods of analysis you might have used, or other explanations you might want to add. When you are satisfied with your conclusions, talk out your findings with the interviewer, step by step, in a clear and concise manner. Begin by restating the question(s) and then follow with your answer(s), outlining the methods you used to arrive at your conclusions. Acknowledge other possible answers and analytical methods, and explain why you have ruled them out or why your chosen method is preferable to the others.

As you might have discerned, "case" interviews can be both challenging and stressful, but they also can be practiced and prepared for. In order to prepare yourself properly for this challenge, we advise you to form or join a "case-prep group" well before the process begins, to afford you the time you need to develop and practice your skills in this new and unfamiliar arena. If such groups are not already forming at your school, ask several friends if they are interested in getting together once or twice a week for practice sessions. Set a regular meeting time and have each member collect sample "case" questions, which should be readily available in the library or career-planning office. You should also be able to find a lot of information on case preparation, along with sample questions, on business school and consulting company websites on the Internet.

Each group member should compile a list of analytical tools to be used in the analyses—most of which will come from your first-year management-strategy and finance courses. You may find it helpful to create a "cheat sheet" of analytical tools to use as a reference in your early days of practicing cases. Before the real interviews begin, however, you'll want to be familiar enough with each of these tools and their application that they are committed to memory.

Once you've set up a schedule, it's practice, practice, practice. At each meeting, pair off and run mock interviews. After each interview, your groupmates should provide you with constructive feedback about your performance, and share with you any analytical pathways you forgot to address, as well as possible alternative ways of looking at the problem. Without this kind of feedback, you won't learn anything from, the experience so be sure to concentrate on giving and getting such feedback.

"Case" questions typically fall into one of a number of common categories, including marketing, cost-benefit analysis, profitability analysis, supply/demand and market share, market-sizing, and others.

"There are a number of great 'case-prep' books out there," Kanna advises. "Just buy one and work through it with your group, and you'll be fine."

The "Good Cop/Bad Cop" and Modern Day "Glued Window" Scenarios

Although it is becoming increasingly uncommon, some old-school firms still employ incendiary tactics during an interview to try to rattle you and throw you off your game. In some instances you may find yourself confronted by two interviewers, one of whom (intentionally—though this is not known to you at the time) will treat you badly, put you in an uncomfortable scenario, or even make controversial or unprofessional comments to you. You may confront the "cold-bench" interviewer who asks you nothing and waits for you to carry the conversation on your own. You may even confront an interviewer who presents factually inaccurate information about the firm during your interview and waits to see if you pick up on it and challenge the misrepresentation.

These modern-day "glued-window" tricks (named after the trick of a generation ago, where the interviewer would ask the interviewer to perform a menial task, such as opening a window, only to find himself unable to do so because, unbeknownst to him, the window had been intentionally glued shut) are arranged to see how you react in uncomfortable situations, how well you can manage your emotions, and how you handle and react to pressure. If you find yourself faced with a situation in an interview that just "doesn't seem right," chances are you're in the middle of a "glued-window" scenario.

Manage your emotions, and get through it.

THE INFORMAL RECRUITING PROCESS

All schools, whether they have a major career-management operations center or not, will notify students of employment opportunities submitted by almost any company. At many schools, this ever-evolving list of job opportunities is available on the school's intranet, which makes it very easy to monitor it daily. Determine how this information is disseminated at your school, since many terrific opportunities to work with smaller and/or rapidly growing companies and other unusual opportunities are often announced in this way.

These opportunities are generally offered by smaller companies seeking one or two summer interns who do not have a formal summer program. If you're looking for a highly structured environment, these positions are probably not for you. Most students who have worked at one of these positions for a summer describe the experience as very entrepreneurial, informal, and requiring much more initiative than the experience of their classmates who went to the larger companies that recruited on campus.

Internships with these types of companies, however, typically offer a lot of contact with senior management and feature a lot of early responsibility. There is also likely to be a lot of flexibility in your job description, which can be good or bad, depending on your perspective. One negative aspect of these internships is that they usually pay considerably less in salary than the larger corporations—although competition for these internships is also likely to be much less significant than for those at the large Fortune 1000 companies.

Applying to any of these smaller companies will require you to manage the application process on your own. There probably won't be a specific due date for cover letters and résumés, but you should apply for these positions as soon as possible after the position is posted, to maximize your chances of success. In your cover letter, inform the company of your plans to follow up with a phone call a week or so after they receive your résumé. This will give you an opening to call the company and find out how the process is going, and it will allow the company to prepare for and expect your phone call, and to determine if they are interested in offering you an interview.

If you are invited to interview, prepare as you would for a formal recruiting interview. Learn as much as you can about the company and the position they are seeking to fill, have some questions prepared, and know your résumé cold.

THE INDEPENDENT JOB SEARCH

The independent job search requires you to research companies on your own, make your own contact with the companies, and set up your own interviews. Students typically engage in this process when their interests are not satisfied by the companies that come to campus during the formal recruiting process. If you go this route, there are several strategies that may significantly increase your chances of success.

First, start your independent job search by determining exactly what it is you're looking to get out of your summer experience. If you want a structured internship with a mentor and one or two specific projects on which to hone your skills, go back to the section on formal, on-campus recruiting and apply to work with a large firm that has an annual M.B.A. summer internship program. If, on the other hand, you are looking to get real, hands-on experience working in a smaller, more entrepreneurial business environment and can handle the ups and downs of a more diverse, flexible job description, you are well suited to undertake an independent job search.

The world of the independent job search essentially has no limits. To prevent the search from becoming completely overwhelming, try to narrow yourself to one or two particular industries (ski equipment, cosmetics), and then to a department (marketing, finance) within that industry. You should then apply any other filters that are important to you (geographic location, company size) to help further narrow your options. Once you have come up with a list of companies that fit your criteria, start networking!

The independent job search is no place for wallflowers or shrinking violets. You will need to target specific businesses, and specific people in those businesses, and then get those people to talk to you and consider offering you a job. This requires persistence, self-confidence, a thick skin, and strong networking skills. You'll need to be prepared to encounter rejection after rejection. Do not let this deter your efforts! The world is full of stories of people who were rejected hundreds of times in a row before being offered the "in" that began their overwhelmingly successful careers.

Use all the contacts you can muster—classmates, professors, old business contacts, alumni, parents, relatives, and anyone else you can think of. You'll be surprised how many people will want to help you, either out of the goodness of their hearts, or to show you how connected *they* are. Don't simply send your materials to a company's human-resources director and then wait for something to happen. If you can't get a better contact at a company, at least follow up with creative, enthusiastic, and persistent appeals to get an audience with the hiring committee. In the game of independent job-seeking, you need to get an audience with a decision-maker at a company who has the authority to make a hiring decision.

"My job search was informal and independent of the school's formal recruiting process. And, to be honest, I was completely on my own. I talked to anyone who would listen and got leads, then followed every lead, had a phone interview, and ended up taking a job that I didn't think I'd like but ended up loving. You just have to remain open to all possibilities and follow up on every loose end. Get your résumé into everyone's hands, and follow up with a phone call. When you are talking to people on the phone, make it an informal interview—ask them how they got to where they are, what they would do differently, and what they recommend that you do. Most people are willing to help. Even if nothing comes of it this time around, you have made a contact to call on the next time as well. Keep a good database of the people whom you have contacted, how you got their names, and what you talked about."

—Alden

Do your homework to determine who the decision-maker is at a particular company, and then do everything you can to get a meeting with that person, or at least to get your materials into his or her hands with an introduction from someone the decision-maker is acquainted with. A cold, written solicitation is easily rejected, but an entrée from someone the decision-maker knows will at least get you serious consideration—and if a job offer is not forthcoming, chances are some additional help, further contacts, or an entrée into a different company will be offered. The old saying about "six degrees of separation" generally holds: The more people you talk to and solicit contacts from, the closer you will get to the "good lead" that can put you directly in touch with the decision-maker you're trying to reach, and the type of job you're looking to land.

> "I focused on some of the Silicon Valley tech giants once on-campus recruiting subsided, and in the end landed a job with Intel. To get this job, I networked at business school, ultimately tracking down the name of an internship coordinator from a second-year student who had worked at Intel the summer before. This coordinator turned out to be very friendly and helpful, and made certain that my résumé got in front of the hiring managers offering positions best-suited to my interests. The entire process progressed quickly and smoothly from there! The best advice I can provide is to not fall victim to the herd mentality. If all of your classmates seem to be vying for the investment-banking and consulting jobs, that does *not* mean you should be doing the same. If you're not pleased with the positions available, then blaze your own trail!"
>
> —Brett

If you engage in an independent job search, it is even more critical to use a spreadsheet or other organizational system to manage the process. Because you are pursuing companies in industries that did not recruit you, you may end up with a large list of companies and contact persons. If past experience holds, less than half these companies will consider hiring a summer intern—so if you are putting all your eggs in the independent job-search basket, be sure your initial list is long enough to account for these odds, and to ensure a reasonable likelihood of success. Organization, including keeping a detailed database, will help you track the companies you've contacted, the substance of your communications with those companies, and where your application process stands with each one.

Since most companies you will communicate with in an independent job search are likely to be smaller, entrepreneurial companies, they may also be less able to predict their summer needs ahead of time. While you might want to start organizing and networking before winter break, you may discover that most of the companies you have targeted won't commit to speak with or interview you until March or April. This can be very disconcerting since most of your friends will be interviewing and accepting offers in January and February. Try not to panic. If you keep talking with people, networking, following up on leads, and stay positive, you will get your break.

In a nutshell, an independent job search is a challenging and extensive puzzle of networking and salesmanship. If you are persistent, however, your efforts will likely be rewarded—and the upside of getting in on the ground floor of a young company with a successful business plan can be extraordinary.

SHUNNING THE "GUNNER" MENTALITY

The "gunner" metamorphosis typically begins with the posting of the first "closed-list" interviews. Suddenly your friends and groupmates inevitably start to compare closed-list interview invitations—a situation that can instantly breed resentment and bitterness. There is only one way to avoid getting sucked into this ugly scene.

Refuse to engage.

Don't ask your classmates or groupmates which companies they are interviewing with, and refuse to discuss your own interview list. It's a no-win situation. If the person you're talking to has more closed-list interviews than you do, you may feel inadequate and start to question your own aptitude. If, on the other hand, you have more interviews, you'll make the other person feel that way, and he'll resent you for it.

Recruiting is a highly personal process by which you seek out the job that best suits you as an individual. Getting four closed interviews in a particular field that is of paramount interest to you, may—for you—be "doing better" than getting ten closed interviews in a broad field would be to the next guy, who really has no idea what he wants to do. It's not about quantity, or even about getting interviews with the "big-name" companies. It's about finding the job that is the right "fit" for you—and that particular calculus is different for everybody.

Don't get drawn into the scorekeeping that goes on during the recruiting process. Nothing will ruin your day, or your reputation, faster. If someone asks you, just tell the person, politely, that you consider recruiting to be a personal matter you'd rather not discuss, and leave it at that.

Oh, there's one more thing:

Once first-round closed interviews are completed, the stress level is ratcheted up another notch as the more paranoid first-year students start comparing who got through the first round and invited on fly-backs or to second-round interviews. As you proceed through the process, questions will become even more direct, ending with how many offers you received, what your salary and bonus package offers were, and what perks were included.

There will always be someone who did "better," and someone who did "worse" in the recruiting process than you did, as defined by money, perks, and prestige. Of course, those criteria don't measure subjective things like how well a job offer "fits" your interests, and thus how happy you'll be once you start working—which is what makes all of these comparisons ridiculous. Keep your own counsel during these crazy times; keep your eye on your own personal goals; and forget about what everybody else is doing.

13

Taking Stock of Your Progress: Exams, Projects, and Papers

"If there is no struggle, there is no progress."
— FREDERICK DOUGLASS

GENERALLY, business school exams will seem quite similar to those you had in college, both in frequency and format. In many classes you will have a midterm and a final, though the midterm could be replaced by a case or another project. Each exam lasts a few hours, and most will be "closed-book," although you may be permitted to bring in a crib sheet of formulas for reference purposes.

PREPARING FOR EXAMS

Your preparation for business school exams will be similar to the approach you took for undergraduate exams. Allow yourself enough time to review and study your notes from class, problem sets, and case studies. If your school permits it, try to get and study copies of your professor's old exams and model answers, as your exam is likely to be very similar. You may also find it helpful to study with your groupmates. Doing so will force you to begin preparations early enough to present your subject matter to the study group. It can expose you to different ways of analyzing a case or applying a theory, and will help you reach consensus on what material is most important.

"I split my time between group and independent studying," Amy recalls. "Independent study enabled me to identify what I didn't know. Spending time with groups enabled me to work through what I didn't understand, and to teach what I thought I did. Nothing lets you know if you understand a topic better than trying to teach it!"

"Make summary sheets or 'cheat sheets' even if you aren't allowed to use them in the exam, because just making them will help you to assimilate the information," Alden adds. "Redoing old problem sets can help, too, since the exam questions are often similar in style and format."

"Most in-class exams are free-response," Brett notes. "Many of my professors, as part of their respective course packets, included copies of previous years' examinations, which serve as excellent preparatory material. You can also benefit greatly from the advice of students who took the same courses with the same professor the year before, who are generally willing to offer their perspectives on how to prepare."

"For quantitative classes, I found that exams were about execution and not about theory," Toby advises. "Therefore, spend the majority of your time practicing problems. I found it helpful to actually write out in words the steps required to solve certain problems, and then to practice solving them."

"My only additional bit of advice," Brett adds, "is to put in the necessary amount of preparation, particularly in your first semester. Many of my classmates had strong academic records, and erroneously concluded they could outperform their business school peers with minimal studying. These students quickly came to realize the caliber of their classmates, and revised their study habits accordingly."

Take-home exams

Although not all schools permit them, take-home exams are, as the name suggests, exams designed to be taken at home. These exams are based on the honor system, and students are trusted to abide by the stated rules of the exam, including its duration and permitted materials. Do not be lulled into complacency by the fact that you have one or more take-home exams. Study for them in the same manner as you would for an in-class exam, since take-home exams—particularly those with longer time limits—are often considerably more difficult than in-class exams.

"You have to nail a take-home exam, because everyone is going to turn in great work," Dave notes. "Having good lecture notes is usually the key to most take-home exams."

Be prepared for this!

Group projects

Group projects in business school are usually assigned to groups of two to six people. Projects can involve analyzing a case, writing a business plan, preparing a marketing strategy, and more. These large assignments, designed to be a practicum for course material, can either take the place of, or be assigned in addition to, a midterm or final.

"If your grade is based on a final group project, break up the tasks and work on the sections individually," Dave suggests. "And set an agenda for when the drafts of each of these tasks are due. Hold people accountable to turn in their parts on time, and once everything is in place, be sure to leave time for two or three more meetings to revise and edit the entire document or project."

"As we assigned discrete tasks to individuals or teams within the overall group, I deliberately took on those responsibilities best aligned with my strengths and interests. If other team members actively competed to take on the same responsibilities, I picked my battles carefully and stuck to my guns only when I felt particularly strongly about owning particular tasks," Brett adds.

Papers

Chances are you will have few analytical "papers" to write in business school. Most business school writing assignments take the form of case analyses, or the preparation of a business plan.

Professors will, however, often have you write short weekly or biweekly "think pieces" on the application of course subject matter to current events. The purpose of these assignments is to apply the theories learned in class to modern business scenarios, requiring an aptitude to work with the theories themselves, and to search for, identify, and understand their appearance and application in "the real world." To more cynical students, these papers are the professors' way of using their students to help them stay current with developments in their disciplines, and to develop new ideas for their publications.

Case studies

Business school is infamous for its use of case studies. Although you will have mastered the art of the case study long before you graduate, they can be intimidating to the uninitiated first-year student.

Generally, a "case study" is a paper that describes a business scenario or situation and provides background information about the company and individuals involved. There are almost always several exhibits attached that provide company financial information and industry statistics. There are typically several questions at the end of the case for you to answer. Your job is to answer them as best you can, with the information provided and, if permitted, with some extracurricular research of your own.

Sometimes you will need to hand in your case analyses, and on other occasions you will just need to be prepared to discuss them in class.

How to tackle a case.

First of all, put your pen down, turn off your laptop, and *read*. On your first read-through of the case, just read . . . as if you were reading a story in a magazine. Allow the facts and figures to wash over you, and just try to get the gist of what is being presented. Resist the urge to write anything down, and just read the thing through to the end, including the questions.

Okay. Once you've done that, go ahead and pick up your pen and give in to your desire to write all over the thing. Make notes in the margins where applicable, and circle relevant facts and figures so you don't overlook anything. As you reread the questions, jot down any initial "gut" thoughts you may have.

Now run the numbers. Input the relevant data into a spreadsheet and start crunching. If you are missing important data (which often happens), make reasonable estimations for the missing data, and be sure to both explain and defend those estimations in your conclusions.

Run three different scenarios for the case: an aggressive scenario, an average scenario, and a conservative scenario. This will give you the range of possible results you'll need to help you evaluate the opportunity in your conclusion.

Finally, use the data, any pertinent analytical tools, and marketing methodologies to draw a conclusion and defend your answer. Finally, provide an alternative—particularly if your analysis results in a conclusion that is contrary to the desired result.

Case studies force you to apply the theories and knowledge you've been learning to real-world scenarios. They are a way to help keep you tethered to the ground, and to understand how what you are learning will be of practical use to you in the business world.

GRADES

Yup. Sad to say it: For all the practical knowledge and experience that you'll get in business school, it is still *school*, and that means that at most schools, your performance will be graded.

Cheer up, though. Business school grading is much more laid-back than grading was in college. At most business schools, it is hard to get anything other than a B. This, of course, has its pros and cons. On the positive side—because it's difficult to do really poorly—the transition back into the educational environment is less stressful and should help you relax and engage the material. On the negative side, however, it's difficult, similarly, to do really well. This has more of an impact than you think—especially in a highly competitive hiring season in times of slow economic growth. With the majority of students receiving Bs, it is difficult to stand out academically. You have to work very hard to receive As in business school, and "gunning" for grades can adversely affect your relationships with your classmates, who, remember, will be your future contacts in the business world. As such, the quest for grades is a delicate balancing act.

What are grades based on?

In general, grades are derived from some amalgamation of your performance on exams and projects, class participation, and, on some occasions, peer/group evaluations. How each of these aspects impacts your final grade is ultimately left to the discretion of each professor. Though your grades on exams, projects, and cases will contribute the greatest percentage to your final grade, professors may leave anywhere from 5 to 25 percent of your grade up to class participation and peer/group evaluations.

Do not make the fatal assumption that the portion of your grade for class participation and/or peer evaluations won't have an impact on your final grade that is significant enough to worry about. Professors include these methods of evaluation for a reason, and in classes with closely bunched exam scores or project grades, that final percentage can swing you up or down by a full grade.

On the importance of getting good grades.

The grades you receive during the first semester of your first year are much more important than those you will earn at any other stage of the experience. First-term grades have the greatest impact on your pursuit for employment because they are likely to be the only grades available during recruiting season. As such, other than your work experience prior to business school, employers will only have your first-term grades on which to evaluate your résumé.

Though it seems ludicrous that the grades from your first term of business school—a time when you are readjusting from the business world back into the academic environment (and are probably experiencing a renewed social life as well)—play the largest role in determining whether you get a summer job, that's just the way it is. Furthermore, because the summer position you choose will greatly impact which employers pursue you for permanent positions after your second year, the importance of your first-term grades is even further magnified.

Take your first term seriously. Take a reasonable schedule, work hard, stay focused, keep up, and don't overcommit to other things. At the same time, though, resist the urge to be a "gunner" for grades. Hard work and focus in business school will bring you the results you seek.

14

Charting Your Course in Business School

"Ordinary people think merely of spending time.
Great people think of using it."

— UNKNOWN

A S NOTED EARLIER, some business school programs assign the
entire first-year curriculum, while others allow students to
choose their classes after the first term or trimester. In a world of
so many classes and so little time, students are frequently caught
up in a struggle about which classes to take.

To help manage your course-selection process at business
school, start by going through the course list as soon as you get
it, and create a spreadsheet or a list of the required classes you
still *need* to take, and all the other classes that you'd *like* to take.
For each class on your list, include the professor, time slot, any
required prerequisites, the expected workload, number of credits,
what major the class contributes to, and any other relevant notes
or information. Having all of this information gathered in one
place will help to bring your course selection choices into sharper
focus—which can be a big help, especially if you are at a school
where bidding for seats in certain classes is competitive.

CORE CLASSES

Your first priority should be to satisfy all "core" class require-ments—by the end of the first year, if possible. Completing the core curriculum early not only will open up your second year to electives, it will provide you with the necessary background to get more out of those electives. It will also assure that you have the nec-essary skills to perform competently in your summer internship.

Completing the core curriculum in this manner may not leave you with a lot of flexibility in your first year, but placing out of one or two core classes can remedy that problem and provide you with more flexibility. At schools where bidding for courses is more competitive and where completing classes provides you with more "currency" to bid with, adopting the "all-core" first-year strategy (where you are less likely to face stiff competition for spots) can put you in prime position to bid strongly for your most desired electives during the second year.

PROFESSOR REPUTATION

Professors' teaching reputations should be one of your paramount considerations in determining your class schedule. Whether you are enrolling in a core class or a high-level marketing elective, be sure to carefully consider the student evaluations of the professor teaching the class. As we have suggested before, a gifted professor can make even the driest subject interesting, and, unfortunately, a bad professor can ruin even the sexiest subject.

Many schools have implemented a system cataloguing student evaluations of professors. Typically, these evaluations are culled from anonymous student surveys gathered in every class at the end of each term—critiquing such things as the professor's teaching skills, method, and style, and substantive, course-related issues like workload, exam type, and paper requirements. This information is then made available to students on the school's intranet or in published form. These evaluations are an invaluable resource, and can provide a critical preview of a course before you enroll.

When considering any course in a school with one of these systems, determine which professors are teaching the class in the upcoming term, and then examine each professor's record. As is true in all areas of academia, the professor can make or break your experience—so don't just go for the "big names" or the convenient course times. Look for the good teachers!

In schools where such a system is not yet available, spend the time to create a thumbnail system of your own. Talk to several second-year students and ask their opinion of the professors that teach the various courses you are likely to take during your time in business school. A little effort in advance can pay significant dividends.

COURSE OFFERINGS AND TIME SLOTS

Core classes and more popular electives are likely to be taught on several different days and times each term. As you get farther along, and into higher levels or more esoteric, specialized subject matter, however, classes may be offered only once a year and at only one time. By and large, teaching schedules do not change drastically from year to year, so you can plan ahead and at least get a sense of when and by whom a class will likely be offered, by looking at any one year's course-selection book. Become familiar with the classes you might be interested in taking during your second year. If a class is offered only once a year, you'll need to be aware of that fact in order not to miss the opportunity.

Resist the urge to take courses based on the time they meet.

You won't enjoy a boring course with a lousy professor just because it meets at ten A.M. on Tuesdays and Thursdays. In the end, it will still be a boring course that you have to drag yourself to each week. Pick the professors, not the course times!

MAJOR REQUIREMENTS

Although you probably will not be required to choose a major until the beginning of your second year, you should begin *considering* a major as soon as possible—ideally, before you even enroll.

How, you ask, are you supposed to know this before you even get to business school?

If you have followed the instructions of the earlier chapters of this book, you should have applied to business school with a specific set of career goals and a specific idea about how your business degree would further those goals. With that information in hand, you should have a pretty good idea about what areas of concentration will best advance your goals.

If you're still not certain, start by eliminating those majors that are of no interest to you. Then become familiar with the course and credit requirements for each of the remaining majors. You will find that the number of required courses and credit requirements vary across majors, and that some courses do double or triple duty in satisfying the requirements of several majors. Often, looking at the titles and descriptions of the various courses required for the majors remaining on your list can help focus your decision-making and help you to select the major that most interests you.

Finally, when choosing your classes, you should always be aware of which and how many classes you still need to satisfy the requirements for your major, and when and at what times these classes are or will be offered. Many an unwary student has ended up with too few credits; missed a required course scheduled only once a year; or scheduled himself into a corner, greatly complicating his ability to earn a major.

"I took the courses I needed for concentrations in Nonprofit Management, Public Management, and Strategy," Alden recalls. "Outside of that, I took courses that had great professors and were recommended by second-year students as classes not to be missed. Generally, once you finish your concentration and take all the courses you feel are relevant to your future, there isn't a whole lot of time left!"

"Before I even began the application process, I knew I wanted to study finance," Brett remembers, "and my conviction only increased through my first year in business school. So, as the auction began for second-year courses, I bid most aggressively on the finance classes of interest to me, and scattered my remaining points among popular courses in other subjects."

PREREQUISITES/CO-REQUISITES FOR FUTURE CLASSES

After reviewing the course handbook, you will likely have discovered several elective classes that are of significant interest to you. When you find classes like this, keep two critical things in mind. First, determine whether the class counts toward your selected major. If it doesn't, make sure the elective doesn't conflict with one of your required courses—or, if it does, that you can make up that required course at another time. Second, determine whether the elective has any prerequisite or co-requisite classes. You may find that in order to take your desired elective, you have to take another class either beforehand or concurrently.

Remember that this is not college. You have only two years in business school, and the first year is primarily consumed with required "core" classes. You need to plan carefully and be aware of all course requirements in order to give yourself the best shot at getting the classes you want.

WORKLOAD

Determine, and then thoughtfully consider, the potential workload for each of the classes you are considering. You do not want to end up with four or five classes that have inordinately heavy reading loads in a single term, nor do you want to end up with five classes that each require a paper a week. Try to select classes with a range of expected workloads and different course requirements, to give yourself a manageable amount of work and some variety each week.

You can get a good idea of the potential workload in a given class by consulting prior student reviews or by looking at the course syllabus, which is typically stored on your school's intranet. As with everything else, students who have taken the class in previous terms are always a good resource.

IMPACT ON SUMMER INTERNSHIP OR CAREER CHOICE

If you manage to complete your core requirements early and have availability for an elective or two in your first-year schedule, give some serious thought to your summer plans when selecting your elective courses. Taking a well-placed elective not only can enhance your summer experience, it can provide you with the knowledge and experience you need to distinguish yourself from the other first-year students vying for the same positions after graduation. For example, if you know you'll be spending the summer at an investment bank, focus on upper-level finance courses. If you'll be spending your summer in brand management, however, look for advanced marketing courses.

"As someone who knew he was trying to get into private equity, I felt it was important to take a number of courses on this subject, and others that were somehow relevant to my career," Matt notes.

FRIENDS AND GROUPMATES IN CLASSES

Once you've narrowed your list of classes for the next term, researched professors and class times, and considered the purpose and impact of taking a particular class, compare notes with your friends and determine if any of your class selections overlap. Having a friend or two whom you know to be diligent and reliable in each of your classes can aid you in more easily forming strong and cohesive work groups.

Note that we *did not* say to pick the classes your friends are taking. Choose your classes first, based on all of the important factors we've already discussed—*then* see if you have any overlap.

NUMBER OF CREDITS REQUIRED FOR GRADUATION

To determine the number of credits you should be taking each term, determine the total number of credits required for graduation and the minimum and maximum number of credits you are permitted to take each term. At the beginning of your first term, you should determine the average number of credits you need to take per term in order to complete the requirements. Briefly map out each of the upcoming two years and allocate credits for each term. This will give you a rough estimate of what each term should look like.

Though you may be tempted to load up on required courses in early terms so that you can maximize your ability to take electives, or just load up in every term in order to get the biggest bang for your tuition buck, resist the urge to become overextended—especially in your first term. Start off by taking the average number of credits and see how it feels.

At least for the first term, give yourself a chance to get adjusted to the demands of business school and to determine the time commitment required to fulfill your obligations to your groupmates and your extracurricular activities. If you find that you have extra time on your hands, you can always add to your workload in future terms. The risks associated with overextending yourself through an overzealous first-term schedule, however, are significant—and much harder to overcome.

15

The Keys to Ascension:
The Summer Internship Survival Guide

"It's not so much how *busy* you are,
but *how* you are busy . . .
the bee is praised, the mosquito is swatted."
— MARY O'CONNOR

SUMMER INTERNSHIPS COME in all shapes and sizes, and will vary dramatically, depending on the position you choose and the size of the firm you work at. If you are headed to a large, multinational corporation, you will likely be surrounded by numerous other first-year business school students and be part of a large and well-organized summer internship program. If your chosen destination is a smaller company, however, you may be one of only a few, or even perhaps the only, summer intern.

Large corporations will have recruiting coordinators responsible for placing you on projects, and who will generally manage and troubleshoot your summer experience. The recruiting coordinator is also likely to be a font of knowledge about the firm. As such, problems that come up during your internship, questions about the firm, and issues regarding procedures at the firm, are best targeted to the recruiting coordinator.

Smaller companies are unlikely to have an official recruiting coordinator or even an official summer "program," per se. As such, if you take an internship at one of these companies, you will need to be more flexible and willing to roll with the punches. It's fairly likely that when you arrive, your employer will not yet know which project or projects you will be staffed on, what work you will be assigned, or who you will be working with. Don't take this personally! Smaller companies are by their nature less structured and more organic, and their focus is likely to be on the day-to-day operations of their organization rather than on building a good summer experience for you. At a small company, building a good summer experience is often your own responsibility.

WHEN YOU ARRIVE

Your first few days at a large corporation will be consumed largely by some form of orientation. You will meet your fellow "classmates," who will likely come from a variety of business schools and many parts of the world. You will also be introduced to your department and the project teams you'll be working with, and provided with an office. Carry a notebook or PDA with you throughout the orientation process to capture important notes about protocol, and names and phone numbers that might come in handy later on.

While your days will be filled with orientation, your nights will likely be booked with social events, including everything from cocktail parties and formal dinners to baseball games and rock concerts. This "wining and dining," which will continue throughout the summer, is the firm's overt attempt to "woo" you as much as possible before you return to school. During the first week or two, you should make every effort to attend all of these social events. The early events, in particular, present the best opportunities to get to know and develop relationships with your fellow summer interns and many of the firm's full-time employees and upper-level managers—who generally make an extra effort to attend the early-summer events as a showing of solidarity and firm unity. Don't be afraid to introduce yourself to these people—that's the purpose of these events! The company managers want to get to know you on a personal level, but they can't do that if you don't talk to them. Resist the urge to be a wallflower, or to seek your comfort zone by hiding out in a small group of other summer interns. Show your interest and commitment to the firm by making introductions on your own. If you are worried about being labeled a "suck-up" for doing this, then bring the managers you meet over to your group of interns so everyone can be involved in the conversation.

If you are starting a summer internship at a small firm, there may be no formal orientation to speak of. Your first day will probably be filled with signing payroll forms, an informal tour of the office, and some informal introductions—but don't wait around expecting a welcoming cocktail hour. Real work may begin almost immediately, if the firm is organized; or, if not, it may appear that the firm has no idea what to do with you.

"By the end of my first day, it was clear that my department had not planned for a summer intern," Brett recalls. "I was disappointed, but at the same time I viewed the group's lack of preparation as an opportunity to forge my own path. I spent the next few days scoping out my department, and over the next week, held a series of meetings with my peers and my manager to define my summer objectives. My colleagues responded very well to my taking initiative, and accommodated my suggested work plan with very few modifications."

Your first few days at a smaller firm may feel very lonely. Hopefully, someone in charge of the summer "program" will make an effort to show you the local lunch spots or invite you to tag along with them, but it is not unusual to find yourself braving it on your own. If you feel isolated, make the effort to introduce yourself to the people around you, and try to hook into some part of the firm's culture. If the firm is not making sufficient efforts to integrate you, then you need to take steps to integrate yourself. Own your experience—and be proactive! In smaller firms, much of the responsibility for the value of your summer experience will depend on your own efforts.

Managing your workload.

No matter the size of your firm, you will need to consciously manage your workload and the type of work you are given. You don't want to appear to be a slacker, but you also want to avoid becoming the person who "can't say no" to work, who then ends up with more assignments than can reasonably be handled, disappointing everyone. There are, however, right ways and wrong ways to go about managing your workload.

At the larger firms, your workload may be effectively controlled by the recruiting coordinator or by your advisor or immediate supervisor. If this is the case, you may not need to do much in order to manage your workload. In this ideal world, your firm and/or work team will have laid out distinct projects for you to work on for a particular amount of time, and nothing else will interfere with that schedule.

Yeah. Get real.

In the real world, you may find you've been assigned to several superiors who don't necessarily communicate with each other about the work they're assigning you. In this case, you will have no choice but to step up and take an active role in managing your workload. Though it may be intimidating, you will need to communicate actively with each of your assigning superiors about the work you have been given, and the deadlines set for that work by each of them. If you begin to get overwhelmed by projects and co-extensive deadlines, it is certainly preferable to be up front and to notify each partner of the requests made by the others, and to explain the impact each partner's request may have on the others' deadlines.

Do not allow yourself to be "brushed off" during these critical conversations. Express a willingness to work hard, but encourage the partners competing for your time to talk with each other, work out their conflicts, and provide you with a reasonable set of marching orders. In extreme cases, or when dealing with difficult personalities, you may need to involve your advisor, the recruiting coordinator, or the human-resources person at your firm to help resolve the conflict. Whatever you do—*do not* allow yourself to get "caught up" in a power play between partners and be forced to take on more than you can handle. Disappointing both partners will only affect one person.

You.

Having said all of that, it is also a mistake to "overmanage" your workload. As the low person on the corporate ladder, you should be willing to step up to the plate and work hard, even to the point of putting in some extra hours on nights and weekends to help resolve backlogged projects and other emergencies. *Do not* tell the partners at your firm that you can't handle your workload if you're working only forty hours a week. In the rough-and-tumble world of business, your definition of what is "comfortable" or "reasonable" might not be the same as the industry standard. The balance lies in being willing to accommodate reasonable requests, while not taking on impossible deadlines or working yourself into the ground.

If you are spending your summer at a smaller company, be prepared for a lot less organization. In a perfect world, you will be assigned to work for only one person, and he or she will always be aware of how much work you have on your plate. In the experience you are likely to have, however, you may face the same "multiple masters" problem just discussed. Handle this circumstance the same way—by explaining your situation to all the people you are working for, making them all aware of the different deadlines you have, and asking them to talk with each other to establish reasonable revised timelines for completing their projects. Establishing an open line of communication with everyone will help resolve the problem, and will show the partners that you are a responsible and proactive member of the team who is interested in the well-being of the whole. Making these efforts takes on added importance at small companies since you may not have a recruiting coordinator to act as a last line of defense to protect you.

It is also more likely at a smaller firm that your assignments will change more rapidly. Smaller companies have fewer personnel among whom to spread new work. Your firm's addition of a new client will require new staffing, and may cause your responsibilities to change. Be aware of this possibility, and try to be flexible. Unless a new project is radically divergent from your skill set or your career objectives, accept the new project with enthusiasm. New assignments lead to new project teams, and more than a few successful careers have begun through such serendipity. Don't be too quick to make a fuss about reassignments, lest you complain your way right out of a golden opportunity!

The key to managing your workload in any job, whether at a large multinational firm, or at a small, entrepreneurial company, is *communication*. Nothing will change if all you do is complain to your friends and co-workers about whatever situation you find yourself in. If, however, you politely and respectfully make scheduling issues known to the partners involved—your advisor, your supervisor, or the recruiting coordinator—you will likely both achieve a resolution and come out of the situation with an enhanced reputation.

Getting the work you want.

The first step in getting the type of work you want, whether you're at a large corporation or a small firm, is to discuss your expectations before you accept the job. During your interviews, or perhaps after you receive your offer, speak with the recruiting coordinator, or the person hiring you, about the skills and knowledge you hope to develop and gain from the internship. Ask direct questions about whether the firm is in a position to accommodate your interests, and whether your expectations match up well with the work the company is planning for you. Although the company's needs may change either before you arrive or during your internship, making the firm aware of your interests and expectations up front makes it much more likely that, if you are hired, the firm will work hard to accommodate you.

"I was very aggressive, but made certain not to overstep my boundaries," Andy says. "There were many opportunities to add value in my department, so I simply asked around to identify those projects that were best aligned with my interests and objectives for the summer. I felt 100 percent responsible for making my internship a success, and took the necessary actions to shape a great learning experience."

"My goal was to learn as much as possible over the twelve-week period. Thus I quickly learned who the best managers were and tried to get assigned to projects specifically with them. I also tried to be very social and outgoing in an attempt to get to know everybody, and for the staff to get to know me. It was a fast-paced environment and I was required to learn a lot very fast. I had spent a lot of time preparing by reading industry literature specific to the fields where I would be working. If I could do it again, I would try to get deal-specific background information on the transactions that I became involved in. That would have saved me a lot of time."

Upon your arrival, remind the recruiting coordinator and your advisor again of your goals and expectations, and discuss the projects they are planning to staff you on. If the projects don't sync up with your areas of interest, probe them gently on why this is so. If it was an oversight, if they forgot what your interests were, or if you failed to previously express them, it may still be possible for the company to reassign you to projects more consistent with your interests—or at least to be on the lookout for future assignments in the areas you hope to explore. If the company's immediate needs have dictated your assignments, however, don't push it. For the moment, you'll need to put the company's immediate needs ahead of your own. Nobody likes a prima donna—and your willingness to be a "team player" and to temporarily table your own individual goals for the good of "the team" can be a golden opportunity to impress your superiors. Do this, and you can be sure that when the dust settles, your superiors will find you the work you want.

"Remember that it all comes down to business needs at any point in time," Toby counsels. "That said, make your desires known, but indicate your flexibility and your willingness to be a team player."

Acquitting yourself favorably on the job.

If you are like most business school students, you have already spent some years out working in the "real world." The rules of the road in the business world change infrequently, so keep your own counsel about what has worked for you in the past. Among the things to remember: Genuine enthusiasm and energy are almost universally appreciated, so try to bring those qualities with you from day one. Summer internships are typically only ten to twelve weeks in duration, so view the experience as a "sprint" and work hard from wire to wire. The days will fly by, and before you know it, you'll be settling back into the more relaxing lifestyle of a second-year business school student. While you are on the job, prove to your firm that you are a candidate worthy of a full-time position. Do a reliably solid job on all of your projects. Be a team player. Don't cut corners, backbite, complain about company policies, or make too many waves.

Throughout your internship, network within the company to help build a case for yourself and to gain exposure to some people you may not actually work with, who can later advocate for your hire. Remember that there is a *critical* difference between earnestly building a case for yourself and brown-nosing; taking credit where credit isn't due; and backstabbing your fellow interns. While it should go without saying, perhaps a reminder is well placed here: In business, your reputation is *everything*. Once sullied, it is almost impossible to repair. Think twice before you take any action.

Mindful of the importance of reputation, avoid burning bridges at the company you intern for, even if you are certain you don't want to return there after graduation. Remember that the business community—particularly within a particular industry— is fluid; people move around; and circumstances change. Even if you harbor strong negative feelings toward someone at the firm, or if someone there has treated you harshly, unless the situation is truly egregious, it is generally best to hold your tongue and walk away. Leave with your reputation intact, and resist the urge to make a scene, or to "get even." Remember that you may want someone within the company to provide you with a recommendation for another position.

The business world, like most other fields, has its share of difficult personalities and unsavory characters. It's how you deal with these characters, however, that determines how people view you.

Getting feedback.

Getting feedback on your job performance is very important. You're trying to make a good impression on your employer with the hope of being extended a permanent offer of employment. Few of us, however, are perfect at anything the first time around, and as such, it is how you respond—both immediately and over time—to constructive criticism and suggestions for improvement, that determines your long-term value to the firm. Soliciting feedback communicates to your employer both that you are open to constructive criticism, and that you are interested in ways you can improve your performance—and getting such feedback at regular intervals during the summer will ensure that you have enough time to make the necessary adjustments.

Soliciting feedback will not only help *you* do your job better, it will get the people you work with to actually *think* about your performance. This will force them to take the time to develop an opinion about you and your work. Consequently, when the company is considering you for an offer of full-time employment, people will remember you, your performance, and your eagerness to develop and improve your skills.

Address the feedback issue at the beginning of the summer when you first sit down with your advisor or supervisor to discuss the projects you will be working on. Since many companies do not provide performance reviews to summer interns until the end of the summer, if at all, take it upon yourself to try to alter this practice. Express your interest in receiving regular feedback, and if necessary, ask your advisor if it would be possible to schedule brief, biweekly "checkup sessions," to help you gauge your ongoing job performance.

"Scheduling time each week with your manager to discuss past programs, future plans, and feedback on performance is a great way to take corrective action early in the internship," Amy notes. "It is also critical to interact with the people you work with outside of strictly business discussions. Go to lunch and company social events to develop personal relationships with the people you work with. If you do this, they will feel more comfortable giving you constructive feedback."

If you find that you're not getting feedback even after having this discussion, don't take it personally. People are busy, and everyone has their own priorities and pressures that need immediate attention. Simply wait a day or two after you've completed a project or an assignment for someone, pop your head into the person's office at an opportune moment, and ask for his or her opinion of your work product—and for any suggestions for improvement.

"It's always tough to work for someone who doesn't give you any feedback on the work that you do," Alden admits. "I've found that asking questions like, 'Was that what you were looking for?' or, 'Did that letter have the right tone or contain the right information?' can help to get the conversation started."

Finally, if one has not already been scheduled for you as your internship draws to a close, you should request an exit interview, or a final performance review, prior to leaving the company at the end of the summer. In addition to providing you with constructive criticism that will help you hone your skills and improve your performance at your next position, the meeting will also give you a good idea of your supervisor's opinion of your performance, and may help you get a feel for whether you are likely to be extended an offer of permanent employment.

Confront problem situations immediately.

During your summer internship, you may be faced with some difficult and challenging moments. Most often these problems involve overzealous or hypercompetitive co-workers undermining your work product or spreading false rumors about you in the office. Although these situations can be extremely frustrating and extraordinarily uncomfortable, it is best to confront the offending individual directly, to tell them you are aware of what they are doing, and to try and talk through the issues that underlie the problem in an effort to come to some sort of resolution. Taking the proactive approach often reveals that an easily resolved misperception or misunderstanding is the cause of the problem. If the direct approach does not resolve the problem, having attempted to confront the issue directly, before involving your advisor or the human-resources director, will show leadership skills and reveal you to be a proactive problem-solver.

More serious problems—including experiences of racism, bigotry, or sexual harrassment—should of course be taken up with your advisor or the human-resources director immediately. Try to keep things professional at all times, and to be as objective as possible. Be direct and forceful without becoming emotional or irrational, as neither will advance your case.

"And be *constructive* with any criticism of the company," Amy adds. "A problem solver and team player is valued. A complainer is not. Sometimes the only difference between the two is perception."

"And treat all people at the company with respect," Matt concludes.

PROPER ETIQUETTE

Proper etiquette during a summer internship involves following just a few very reasonable guidelines that you'd think would be self-evident. You'd be amazed, however, at how many people fail to follow these simple edicts with sometimes humorous but disastrous results.

First, there will almost always be an unrestricted amount of alcohol available at company social events. Remember—drink sensibly! Your objective for the summer is to make a strong impression on your employer, and you want to be sure that it is a *positive* impression—based on your work product, attitude, personality, and professional judgment. Earning a reputation, even among your fellow interns, as the biggest partyer, *will not* materially advance your efforts to land a job offer, and may bring the scorn of the more conservative members of your company upon you.

Second, when dining out on the firm at social events, be mindful of what you are ordering. If, for example, a couple of senior managers invite you out for an evening "on the company," do not take advantage of the situation by having four drinks before dinner, oysters Rockefeller, twin lobster tails, and two desserts. The old rule your mother once taught you still applies, folks—even when ordering on the firm's tab. Take your lead from what at least one of the managers had ordered, to get a sense what the parameters are. Once the situation has become more clear, order a meal that is either comparable or less expensive. Failure to observe this universal rule will catch the eye of socially adept managers wary of potential abusers of the expense account. We know of at least one case where someone failed to get a job offer because of repeating this mistake.

During the summer, particularly at large companies, you may be invited to social events several times a week, and often on the weekends as well. As we mentioned earlier, you should make an effort to attend all of the early-summer events, as these events will afford you the best opportunity to bond with your fellow interns and to network with people in the company before key players start disappearing on summer vacations. Once your face is known at the company and you have established a "comfort level" with people there, it is perfectly acceptable to pick and choose the social events you want to attend. As the summer progresses, you'll be able to gauge which events are "command performances" and which ones you can safely miss if you'd prefer to have some time for yourself.

Take responsibility for any errors or oversights that you make during the course of the summer. Be forthright about your mistakes: Report them as soon as possible to the individuals that will be affected by them; apologize; and offer to try and help correct any problems that have flowed from your mistake. Do not try to cover up mistakes, deny involvement, blame someone else, or attempt to downplay or make light of your error. Everyone makes mistakes occasionally—but it is how you deal with making a mistake that shows character. You stand to gain much more from accepting responsibility for mistakes and striving to correct them.

Finally, be *extremely* cautious about starting any romantic relationship with someone at the company. Beginning a relationship with another intern, a secretary, or a superior during a summer internship is riddled with professional risk, and almost always works to your disadvantage. At large firms there are one or two of these intraoffice romances every year, which at best are distracting and, at worst, become the stuff of office folklore. Even if your firm doesn't have a policy forbidding intraoffice relationships, there will inevitably be managers who frown upon the practice, and these people may be influential in deciding your future at the firm. Relationships that break up can be divisive in an office, polarizing people and impeding the ability of those people to work together effectively. Entering into any sort of work relationship is frequently seen as a sign of immaturity and shows a lack of professional judgment. If you are truly interested in a person you meet during your internship, wait until the internship is over to act, and be prepared to seek alternative employment the following year.

WHEN IT'S OVER

Once you've returned to school, maintain an open line of communication with your summer employer. Stay in touch by phone or e-mail with your advisor and the recruiting coordinator. Make clear any genuine eagerness to return to the company after you graduate. If you are certain of your commitment to the firm and are so inclined, you might also offer to work for the company on a project-by-project basis during your second year. Be sure to balance your interest in doing this with the demands of the classes you need to take in order to fulfill a major and graduate; any electives you want to take; and any commitments you have made to extracurricular activities—to ensure that if you commit to a project for the company, you can complete the work promptly and efficiently.

16

Making the Turn:
What Makes This Year Different
from the Last?

"Experience is not what happens to a man;
it is what a man does with what happens to him."
— ALDOUS HUXLEY

A T THE BEGINNING of your first year, if you're like most of us, you were nervous and didn't know exactly what to expect. At the beginning of your second year, your apprehensions about going back and functioning in the academic environment will be replaced with new concerns—like the fact that "the rest of your life" in the post–business school world is now only nine months away.

This realization will likely leave you with two conflicting trains of thought: (1) "I only have nine months left to complete my requirements and learn everything I can that could possibly help me later on"; and (2) "I only have nine months left to enjoy my freedom from the responsibilities of full-time employment and to get my golf game in shape." Ideally you will reach some happy medium on these competing desires. So, as the second year begins, refocus on your goals, research the classes that are available to you, and chart a sensible course for your second year.

"Be sure to take classes that interest you so you stay engaged," Anne suggests.

"The first year of business school is really about trying to get everyone up-to-speed on business basics," says Matt, "while the second year allows you the opportunity to more deeply explore the specific interests you have discovered."

At the same time, though, remember to take advantage of the social opportunities available to you. The second year of business school is basically a nine-month opportunity to network and to build genuine friendships and business relationships that will serve you well through the rest of your career—so don't ignore this vital part of the experience, either!

"The second year is definitely more laid-back," Andy recalled. "For most, the job search during the second year is complete by the fall, and schedules inevitably become a lot more flexible, leaving more time to engage in fun activities, to strengthen your relationships with your peers, and to have a good time."

There are a few other differences between the first and second years of business school that are worth noting. First, you will enjoy a lot more flexibility when choosing your classes. With first-year "sections" now permanently disbanded, you will have control not only of the subjects you take, but the class times, the professors, and your groupmates.

"I think the biggest difference is that, as you enter the second year, the uncertainty you had the year before, which caused a lot of unnecessary stress, is gone," Dave adds.

We have already addressed the importance of choosing professors carefully; do not underestimate the importance of this. A poor professor can ruin even your most highly anticipated class, while a skilled professor can provide you with a solid base of knowledge and a palatable experience in even the driest subject, so take the time to make informed choices.

While the ability and flexibility to choose course times is something to be embraced, too many business school students are shortsighted about this—using the opportunity to create four-day weekends or the option to sleep until noon every day.

Don't be a fool.

"I went to business school to learn, not just to get a job, so I wanted to get the most I could out of my classes," Alden recalls. "Business school is not cheap, and it is an incredible waste to while away the second year. There is plenty of time for extracurricular activities and bonding with your classmates. Find the balance that works for you, but think about how you will look back on your years in business school, and make sure you have no regrets."

Use the flexibility in class times to take the classes and professors you couldn't take before, and follow the design you set for yourself. If you are willing to take classes at unpopular times, you will be able to stretch your currency in the course bidding process a lot farther and, accordingly, end up taking a much higher proportion of the classes you had hoped to take. Chances are, taking this approach will still leave you with a couple of mornings or afternoons every week to play golf. Be mindful, however, that you can play golf for the rest of your life. You will pass through business school but once—and when it's over, there is no going back.

"Second semester of the second year is the most relaxed time in school," Amy observes. "Extracurricular responsibilities are passed off to the first-years, and most recruiting is over. Although my general activity level declined, I got a lot out of the second semester because I took classes that really interested me, and worked as a teaching assistant. Having people depending on me kept me very engaged."

"One can certainly shift into neutral as a second-year M.B.A., particularly after recruiting season concludes," Brett notes. "On the other hand, when you're paying in the neighborhood of $100,000 for a graduate education, why not take advantage of everything the school has to offer? I kept things fresh by loading up on finance courses that interested me, tutoring first-year students in my favorite subjects, and fulfilling my responsibilities as co-head of the volleyball team."

As you are selecting classes and planning a schedule, do not lose sight of the courses required for your major(s), and any pre-requisites needed for more advanced coursework. You only have two terms (or three trimesters) left, so failing to enroll in a required class or prerequisite can be irreparable. Make your list and check it twice.

As a second-year student, chances are that you will also have gained some new responsibilities. You may have been elected the head of a club, or accepted a leadership position in another campus organization. If so, your responsibilities to that organization will carry you through at least the first half of your second year. As the leader of one of these organizations, expect your fall term to be very busy recruiting first-year students, planning conferences and club events, and being occupied with other managerial tasks. Plan accordingly!

Finally, one of the biggest changes between the first and second years of business school is that, for second-year students, recruiting events will begin almost as soon as you return to campus. Interview rounds will begin in October, and the entire process is usually winding down by the end of the fall term. As such, you will need to be prepared to address your employment situation as soon as you arrive back on campus in the fall of your second year. Were you happy enough with your summer internship to commit to that company long-term? Were they happy enough with you to make you an offer of permanent employment? How do you know "for sure" whether the company is a good "fit" for you? You'll need to be thinking ahead about these questions.

The next chapter will walk you through that process.

17

Recruiting in the Second Year: The Quest for Permanent Employment

> "Make yourself indispensible, and you will move up.
> Act as though you are indispensible,
> and you will move out."
> —JULES ORMONT

ALTHOUGH THERE ARE many similarities between recruiting for full-time positions and last year's recruiting for summer internships, there are also several important differences. Like last year, you will need to attend recruiting events, send out applications, and interview with many companies in an effort to find the ideal job. While the overall structure of the process will not change much, there are many new subtleties in the process to be aware of.

First, as we noted in the last chapter, the second-year recruiting process begins almost immediately after you return to campus in the fall. This means you will need to have your application materials (complete with a résumé updated to reflect your most recent summer employment) ready to be filed shortly after you return to school. Plan ahead, and if you know you're going to be entering the second-year hiring pool, prepare as many of these materials as you can before you get back to school.

If you are like most of us, you will find the recruiting atmosphere much more pleasant the second time around. Whether it's

BUSINESS SCHOOL CONFIDENTIAL

because you are more familiar with the process and are used to its rigors; you have an offer in your pocket that you are trying to improve upon; you have worked as a summer intern in the industry in which you are applying and have a better idea of what the company is looking for; or because, having gone through the process once already, you have grown accustomed to harsh interviews and occasional rejections—almost everyone we know found second-year recruiting to be mellower and less outwardly competitive.

Interviews during second-year recruiting are frequently more thorough, and there may be more "rounds" of interviews and more fly-back interviews at company headquarters than there were last year. This is because companies traditionally put more effort and more money into interviewing candidates for full-time employment. A first-year student who is a bad fit can be readily discarded. Second-year interviews, however, end in full-time job offers, and as such, represent a longer-term commitment by the company.

There are also likely to be more small companies recruiting second-year students, which will offer you a greater variety of job options. Smaller companies tend to be less interested in hiring summer interns because interviewing and recruiting consumes valuable time and resources. As such, many small companies make their first appearances in the second-year recruiting process, where they can get more "bang for their buck" by recruiting candidates only for those full-time positions identified as immediate needs.

Figuring out whether to make a second run at recruiting.

The obvious cases are the easiest. You loved the company where you did your summer internship, your interests matched well with the company's hiring needs, and the company made you a great offer for full-time employment after graduation. Hey—congratulations and more power to you! You're done! Every year there is a relatively small percentage of students—around 15 percent on average—that find themselves in this position and do not reenter the second-year recruiting process.

Don't be discouraged, however, if you didn't leave your summer internship with a permanent offer of employment. Many companies, as a matter of course, wait until late fall to extend offers to their previous summer interns in order to be in a better position to gauge their hiring needs. If you do have a strong interest in returning to the company you interned with, maintain regular communication with the recruiting coordinator and your advisor throughout the fall, and be sure to make your sentiments clear. But join the second-year recruiting process in earnest, just in case.

If you don't get an offer of full-time employment from the company you interned with during your first summer, take all possible steps to turn this setback into a positive situation. Ask for feedback regarding the company's decision not to make you an offer. Their decision may have been one of economics rather than one dictated by your performance. If this is the case, inquire whether the recruiting coordinator or your advisor at the company would be willing to provide you with a reference to explain this problem, since the subject *will* come up in your second-year interviews with other companies. Don't walk away from rejection with your tail between your legs! Everyone is rejected from a position sooner or later. Successful people learn how to turn rejections into new opportunities.

Other obvious cases for a return to the recruiting process include students who do a summer internship with a company and find that they really didn't enjoy the work or the corporate culture—and students who discovered during the course of the internship that their interests have changed. Both of these are valid reasons to explore new opportunities more in keeping with your newly identified distinctions.

But what about the closer cases? The case where you really

loved your internship and the corporate culture, but the available position is at a satellite office in a secondary market for a secondary-market–size compensation package? Or the case where your attraction to the position at a particular company is linked to working with one or two key people who are rumored to be looking to leave the company; or the case where something else in your gut tells you you're "just not sure" that the fit at the place of your summer internship is optimal?

"Explain to the company that you want to make as informed a decision as possible," Toby advises, "and that doing so will be beneficial to both you and the company in the long run. When possible, however, work with your summer employer to figure out a realistic date by which you will accept or decline. It is important that you maintain goodwill."

If you come out of your summer internship with an offer that you are less than ecstatic about, with the benefit of that experience under your belt, you need to come up with some way to objectively evaluate what it is that you are looking for in permanent employment. Is it the compensation package that is foremost in your mind? The type of work you'll be doing? The corporate culture and atmosphere? The city?

"If you are lucky enough to have a full-time offer coming out of your summer internship, you have the ability to be selective about which companies you interview with," Toby continues. "While the idea of forgoing second-year recruiting may be very appealing, it's important that you do your due diligence and make sure that there aren't any better opportunities out there for you. This will likely be the last time that companies will be coming to you. If you're not certain, use the time to explore."

Have you even sat down to break out each of the primary factors involved in choosing a place of employment, in order to figure out how important each factor is to you?

No?

Well, then, it's time to go to school!

Economic influences on second-year recruiting.

The state of the economy at the time you are engaged in recruiting will have a significant impact on your success rate and how selective you can be in applying for permanent positions. In the economic boom of the late 1990s, companies were literally throwing themselves at business school students. In those days, students were in the driver's seat, often commanding several offers from top firms and playing them against each other for top dollar. Meanwhile, sexy new entrepreneurial dot-com companies were hiring aggressively from the business school ranks, and employing competitive hiring tactics, forcing more traditional employers like investment banks and consulting firms to work harder to lure their share of M.B.A.s into their ranks. As a result, skyrocketing starting salaries, signing bonuses, and incredible perks of all shapes and sizes were commonplace.

In the dot–bomb-out at the beginning of the new millenium, and in the deep recession that followed, the recruiting environment was much different. Companies plagued by shrinking profits and decreased demand for their products and services began withdrawing from on-campus interview locations they had populated for years, and those that did come hired for many fewer spots than in previous years. In the down market that began this millenium, employers regained control of the marketplace, and students—particularly those at the lesser-ranked business schools—really began to feel the squeeze. New positions were considerably more scarce, and with refugees from the dot-bombs flooding into the "safe haven" of business school, swelling enrollment to record numbers in 2002, competition for the smaller number of jobs became even more fierce. Signing bonuses and other perks like generous relocation expenses, paid car leases, and furniture stipends, dried up. At the ebb tide of the recession, the more desperate companies paid significant stipends to graduating M.B.A.s with employment offers, to look for positions with *other* firms, to *defer* their coming to work for several months—in the hopes that economic conditions at the company would improve, or simply rescinded offers entirely, leaving graduating M.B.A. students actually looking for work.

Suffice it to say, therefore, that the economic times at the time of your job search should animate your strategies at least to some degree. Keep this in mind as you round out your list of potential employers. Even if you are lucky enough to be in business school in a time of a rising or a booming economy, much in the job hunt remains beyond your control. Markets can change while you're in school. Company needs can change, and in the course of the two years you're in school, entire industries can die and others can be born. Try not to get discouraged by the elements and influences that are out of your control. The economy is cyclical, and will always fluctuate. As a business school student, you just need to be aware how the ebbs and flows affect the job market, and prepare yourself as best you can to face the market you draw.

Making employment decisions using the "Relevance Calculus."

Below, you will find a list of thirty-one defined factors that might readily influence your choice of employment. Perhaps there are others you can come up with that are important to your personal situation. Take the time to sit down and work through the following exercise. Figure out what matters most to you in choosing a place of employment, and what factors are less important. We guarantee that if you sit down and spend the half hour or so it takes to complete this exercise, you will learn something, and probably several things, that will help to clarify your job search in your own mind and steer you in the right direction.

First, read the descriptions of the various factors below, and assign each of these factors an "importance value" from "0" to "2" in the space provided in the following chart. Give a factor a "0" if it is of little or no importance to you, a "1" if it is somewhat important to you, and a "2" if it is very important to you. Note that there are several blank spaces intentionally provided in the chart in case you want to write in extra factors.

FACTORS IN THE RELEVANCE CALCULUS

(Score factors (0) "Not Important"; (1) "Somewhat Important"; or (2) "Very Important"—based on their personal importance to you in choosing a job.

NAME OF FACTOR	SCORE
Compensation package	_____
Benefits/Vacation package	_____
Prestige of firm or brand(s)	_____
Length of partnership/Promotional track	_____
Length of typical workweek	_____
Travel schedule	_____
Ability to do type of work desired	_____
Firm training/Mentoring program	_____
Distribution of work/Makeup of work teams	_____
Firm hierarchy/Opportunity for advancement	_____
General employee satisfaction	_____
Corporate culture	_____
"Fit" with other employees/managers at firm	_____
Maternity/paternity policy	_____
Percentage of minority employees/managers	_____
Firm's attitude toward alternative lifestyle choices	_____
Political leanings of company and employees	_____
Social consciousness of company	_____
Desirability of firm's office space	_____
"Perks"	_____
Friends at the company	_____
Potential to move laterally within the industry	_____
Desirability of city where firm is located	_____
Housing options near the office	_____
Length of commute to work	_____

Proximity to family   ————

Proximity to close friends/significant other   ————

Potential to find significant other in this City   ————

Cultural Activities   ————

Nightlife   ————

Proximity to favored hobbies/Outdoor activities   ————

Write in: ————

Write in: ————

Write in: ————

Write in: ————

Deciding where to apply.

With summer experience and an evaluation of the above criteria under your belt, it's time to go job-hunting! As you probably learned last year, the best ways to learn about how particular companies match up with your criteria are by attending recruiting events, talking to classmates who worked at the companies that most interest you, doing some Internet research, and talking with administrators in the career management center.

Once you have worked up a list of the companies and positions that best jibe with your personal and professional goals, again we highly recommend developing some sort of spreadsheet to manage the process. Like the one you might have developed last year, this database should keep track of recruiting event dates, application due dates, the requirements of each of these applications, any communications you have had with people at the company, contact information, and anything else you consider useful. Keeping yourself as well-organized as possible during the recruiting process is imperative.

Finally, we offer a word of caution about finding a balance in the job-hunting process. Do not apply to only three or four companies, no matter how confident you are in your track record. Though you may know that these three or four companies are your "perfect fits," be sure to also apply to the handful of other companies that you targeted as "next-best" options. Remember that needs in the job market in almost any industry can change overnight, and what seemed like a "sure thing" yesterday could be a long shot tomorrow. Be sure to give yourself enough options in the application process to assure yourself of *some* position after graduation. If you fail to land your top-choice position coming out, opt for "the next-best thing." You can always attempt to move laterally later on.

Having said that, you should also avoid gross overapplication for ill-fitting positions simply to assure yourself of having options. Overapplying beyond your areas of real interest is a waste of your time, and can also take interview spots at a company you're barely interested in, away from classmates who would kill to work there. "Flooding the market" with your résumé, especially in areas outside your primary interests, will draw the ire of your classmates and damage your reputation. Take the time to identify the companies and positions of serious interest to you, and apply accordingly. Seek the assistance of your school's career services center if you are having difficulty narrowing your list.

Preparing for interviews.

Preparation for second-year interviews should not be much different from the preparation you did last year. To refresh yourself on the different types of interviews you might encounter and the strategies for success in each, reread chapter 12. Do not assume that because you went through the process last year, you don't need to brush up on your interview skills! At a minimum, your preparation for second-year interviewing should include setting up a videotaped analysis with the career management center (if available), and working with a "case-prep" group to refresh your familiarity with the important success tactics in these interviews. You will probably not need to spend as much time preparing as you did last year when the concept of the "case" interview was new to you—it will probably only take a few practice rounds with your prep group to get you back in winning form . . . but take the time to practice. The first-round "case" interview with your first-choice company is not the time to realize that your "case" interviewing ability has grown rusty.

A refresher on proper interview etiquette.

Although it should go without saying, be sure to exhibit proper etiquette during all your interviews. You'd be amazed to know how many in-hand offers end up getting blown or subsequently withdrawn as a result of students' callous disregard of what you'd think were obvious, bright line rules of etiquette. Remember the following:

- *Never be late to an interview.* Always arrive at your interviews a few minutes early. If the interview is at the company's offices, and you have never been there before, be sure to allow yourself ample time to get there and find your way to the right office.
- *Always be polite, accommodating, and understanding.* Even if your interview is beginning much later than expected and the company seems to have disregarded that you, too, may have a schedule you are trying to keep, smile and let it pass. If you need to reschedule anything because of the delay, excuse yourself from the proceedings for a few minutes and slip away into an empty room where you can make some calls and adjust your schedule accordingly.
- *Turn your cell phone and your Blackberry ringer and vibrator off!* Is there anything more important during an interview than the interview? What were you planning to do, answer the call or write an e-mail during the proceedings?

Unless you are expecting word of the birth of your first-born child, any electronic communication devices you have must be turned all the way off.

- *Dress conservatively.* The business world is still conservative, as a rule. Never arrive at an interview in "business casual" clothing unless you are specifically advised to do so. Remove any unusual piercings, and be understated with your hairstyle, jewelry, and cologne or perfume. Let your résumé, your personality, and your answers to the interviewer's questions do the talking for you.

- *Never let your guard down during an interview!* Even if an interview becomes very informal, remember, it is still an interview. There is never a place for foul language, off-color jokes, or negative remarks about fellow applicants. *Never.*

Choosing a company.

It's time to revisit the factors we discussed in the "Relevance Calculus" above in greater detail. This time, though, we're going to move from the abstract world of, "How much does this factor generally matter to you?" to the concrete world of the factors *as they specifically apply to the various companies you are considering.* Take a look at the list of factors below. This time you'll see we have added some text to help you determine how each factor applies to the companies you are considering.

Just play along. The point of the exercise is just around the bend.

Factors in the Relevance Calculus
- *Compensation package:* Starting salary, including any bonuses, stock options, and relocation expenses the firm will cover.
- *Benefits/Vacation package:* The amount and quality of

health, dental, and life insurance the firm will provide to you; whether your spouse and children are also eligible under the benefits package; number of weeks of paid vacation allowed per year; sabbatical program, if any.

- *Prestige of firm or brand(s):* Overall reputation of firm within its industry.

- *Length of partnership/Promotional track:* The number of years you should expect to work before you could be considered for partnership or a promotion to upper-level management. If there are no rote requirements, ask for averages. Determine whether there are different levels of partnership (junior partner, non-equity partner), and the number of years required to reach each level.

- *Length of typical workweek:* Find out what the average associate billable hours were for the prior year, if applicable; or otherwise, what the typical hours and work week are. Do work teams routinely meet on weekends? Is there pressure to work six- or even seven-day weeks?

- *Travel schedule:* Some people love to travel for work, others hate it. How much travel can you expect to do in this position, and how does that jibe with your preferences?

- *Ability to do type of work desired:* Does the job you are applying for offer the type of experience you are really looking for? Will you be allowed to pick the department or practice group you want to work with?

- *Firm training/Mentoring program:* Will you be assigned a mentor on your work team or in your practice group? What kind of training does the firm provide? Is this going to be a "sink or swim" environment, or can you expect to be brought along more slowly?

- *Distribution of work/Makeup of work teams:* Are assignments filtered to you through an advisor, mentor, or a central clearinghouse, or is the distribution of work more "informal" (*read:* haphazard)? Is there anyone you will be able to turn to when your workload becomes unbearable? For people who have a difficult time refusing assignments, this is a critical question to ask.

- *Firm hierarchy/Opportunity for advancement:* What is the partner-to-associate ratio? Top-heavy firms can be very taxing on associates, since there are only so many people around to field assignments from partners. You might also want to find out how projects are typically staffed. Will it be just you and a partner, or will there also be a midlevel person on the project who can help you over the rough spots? How frequently are promotions made, and what opportunity is there for upward mobility?

- *General employee satisfaction:* How happy are the employees at the firm you are considering? Largely a "gut feeling" here, since you probably only met these people for part of a day, but how did they look? Were they smiling and cordial, or were they generally scowling, walking around with their heads down, looking exhausted? Did they greet each other in the hallways, or just walk past each other like ships passing in the night? Did the people you meet seem to have interests outside the office, or was the office their life? Are these the kind of people you'd want to hang out with socially?

- *"Fit" with other employees/managers at the firm:* More "gut feeling" stuff, but what do you think? Are the people at this firm enough like you that you'll have things to talk about? Would you be comfortable working in a place like this? Is this the kind of place you'd be excited to come to every morning, or do you already feel like you'd have nothing in common with a lot of the people you met? How does your personality and style mesh with the people you'll be working with?

- *Corporate culture:* Is this a "white shoe" firm or company from yesteryear, where "your kind" might appear to be welcome at the front door, but not actually welcome in the back hallways and boardrooms? Is there an obvious "old boys" network at play? Does the company feel more like a college fraternity where boozing and partying after work is overemphasized? Is the place stiff and overly formal? Does it feel cold and austere, or warm and comfortable? First perceptions can be accurate ones.

- *Maternity/paternity policy:* Want to have kids someday but still keep your job? Better find out about this. While you're at it, find out whether the company provides on-site daycare. Some do.

- *Percentage of minority employees/managers:* Want to work in a diverse, or at least nonbigoted, environment? Look around when you visit. What do you see? Does the place look ethnically diverse, or white as snow? Is there a mix of males and females in the partnership? If you have doubts, you'd better ask some questions. Better to find out now than after you start.

- *Firm's attitude toward alternative lifestyle choices:* Are you gay, lesbian, or bisexual? Better investigate what the firm's reaction will be when they find out. Are there any gays or lesbians in the partnership or upper-level management? Is there a nondiscrimination policy in place that includes a clause on sexual orientation? Ask to see the firm's policy.

- *Political leanings of company and employees:* Have a problem with drilling in the Alaskan wilderness? coaxing teenagers to smoke? exploiting labor forces in third-world countries? Believe that a rising tide lifts all boats? Whatever your personal political leanings, how do they match up with your company's priorities? Will you be able to put the company's needs ahead of your own beliefs?

- *Social consciousness of company:* Does your company put social concerns ahead of the bottom line? Do you care?

- *Desirability of firm's office space:* Where is the company's space located? What does the office space look like? Will you have your own office? How big will it be? Completely a matter of personal taste here.

- *"Perks":* Does the company have a luxury box at the arena or the ballpark? Will you ever actually get to use it? Does the firm provide discounted country-club memberships or waived initiation fees? health-club memberships? low-interest home loans? help getting a good mortgage? meals if you are working late? a car to drive you home if you are working really late? errand service? Ask!

- *Friends at the company:* Don't underestimate the importance of having someone you can trust at work. Your job will have its moments, and having someone there to talk to who knows the personalities you are talking about and understands the firm culture can be very helpful.

- *Potential to move laterally within the industry:* If your job at this company ends up being less than you expected, how easy will it be for you to move laterally in the industry from this job? Is your company well known and/or well-respected, and/or will your position leave you with transferable skills?

- *Desirability of city where firm is located:* Do you have a favorable or unfavorable overall impression of the city where the firm is located?

- *Housing options near the office:* Are there affordable and attractive places to live near the office? Ask the younger people at the firm where they live, and for any recommendations. How do these compare to the options in the other cities you are considering?

- *Length of commute to work:* Pretty much speaks for itself, right? Also consider whether you will be traveling via public transportation or driving. Do you prefer one over the other? Are both options available and convenient?

- *Proximity to family:* Can be good or bad, depending on

your family. Whichever one it is, how do you feel about it? Are you close enough to them or far enough away from them to feel comfortable?

- *Proximity to close friends/significant other:* Sure, you'll be meeting lots of new friends, but it helps to have an established network of friends in a new place to get you started—or at least to have a friend or two nearby to call on when times get tough. How far away are your best friends? Where is your significant other? Yes, people try the long-distance relationship thing, and a few of them even manage to make it work for a while. As a young associate at a consulting firm or an investment bank, or as a young manager at a growing company, you probably won't be one of them.

- *Potential to find a significant other in this city:* Hoping to find a nice Jewish boy in Boise? Ever heard of a cowboy named Goldberg? Being single in rural anywhere probably isn't a good idea, either.

- *Cultural activities:* How are the museums and galleries? Is there a live-music scene? Are there good movie theaters? plays? exhibitions? ethnic restaurants and stores?

- *Nightlife:* How is the local bar, club, and music scene? Is it the kind of scene you'd enjoy? How close are the ballparks, stadiums, and arenas? Are there generally seats available to the games, or is every game sold out a year in advance?

- *Proximity to favored hobbies/Outdoor activities:* When the snow starts to fly, how far is the nearest good skiing? How far to the beach, the lake, the mountains? Is there hiking and kayaking nearby? Are there bike and running trails in town? good parks?

If you have done your homework, you should already know where each firm you are considering stands with respect to each of these factors. Just below, you will find the "Relevance Calculus" chart, which will help you to really think about each factor and its importance to you and to your decision. You may want to photocopy this chart several times so you can fill one out for each company you are considering.

Here's how it works.

First, go back to the beginning of this chapter where you assigned each of these factors a number from "0" to "2," depending on its importance to you. Transfer those numbers into the "Relevance Calculus" table below. Now, assign the company you are considering a score from "1" to "5" for each of the factors discussed. For example, on the factor "Compensation package," give a firm a factor score of "1" if the firm's salary and bonus structure is lousy; a "2" if it is below average; a "3" if it is average; "4" if it is above average; and a "5" if it is outstanding.

After you have assigned each factor an "importance" score (0–2), and a "factor score" (1–5), multiply the two scores together to get the "Total Factor Score" for each factor. For example, if you assigned the factor "Compensation package" an importance score of 2 ("Very Important"), and gave a particular firm a factor score of 3 ("average") for "Compensation package," the math for salary and bonuses for that firm would be 2 times 3, for a "Total Factor Score" of 6. Note that if you ruled a particular factor "Not Important," you will end up with a total factor score of 0 for that factor (because you are multiplying by zero).

Complete these calculations for each factor until you have filled the entire table, and then add up the "Total Factor Scores" of all the factors. The number you end up with is the "Final Company Score." Compare the Final Company Scores of each of the firms you are considering, to help you decide between them. Be sure that you can give each company an honest grade on each factor. If you need more information, it's time to get on the horn and start asking some questions.

THE RELEVANCE CALCULUS

Company Name: _____

FACTOR	IMPORTANCE TO YOU 0 = Not Important 1 = Somewhat Important 2 = Very Important	X	SCORE = 1 = Worst 5 = Best	TOTAL Factor Score
Compensation package				
Benefits/Vacation package				
Prestige of firm or brand(s)				
Length of partnership/Promotional track				
Length of typical workweek				
Travel schedule				
Ability to do type of work desired				
Firm training/Mentoring program				
Distribution of work/Makeup of work teams				

FACTOR	IMPORTANCE TO YOU 0 = Not Important 1 = Somewhat Important 2 = Very Important	×	SCORE 1 = Worst 5 = Best	=	TOTAL Factor Score
General employee satisfaction					
"Fit" with other employees/managers at the firm					
Corporate culture					
Maternity/paternity policy					
Percentage of minority employees/managers					
Firm's attitude toward alternative lifestyle choices					
Political leanings of company and employees					
Social consciousness of company					
Desirability of firm's office space					
"Perks"					
Friends at the company					
Potential to move laterally within the industry					
Desirability of city where firm is located					

FACTOR	IMPORTANCE TO YOU 0 = Not Important 1 = Somewhat Important 2 = Very Important	×	SCORE = 1 = Worst 5 = Best	TOTAL Factor Score
Housing options near the office				
Length of commute to work				
Proximity to family				
Proximity to close friends/significant other				
Potential to find a significant other in this city				
Cultural activities				
Nightlife				
Proximity to favorite hobbies/outdoor activities				
Other:				
Other:				
Other:				
Other:				

18

Parting Thoughts

"There will come a time when you believe
everything is finished. That will be the beginning. . . ."

— LOUIS L'AMOUR

SO THERE YOU have it.

Everything you need to know to apply, choose, survive, and thrive in business school, neatly packaged between the covers of this book. But don't let this be the end of your examination of the process.

Talk to people who have gone through the experience. Test our advice against what they tell you. Get advice specific to the particular schools you are applying to—as every school is a little bit different.

"There is no clear recipe for success in the business world," Matt admits. "Many people have made it to the top with little or no formal education, let alone business school. Sometimes all it takes is a good idea and some initiative. But business school can often serve to accelerate a career by providing the contacts, the basic business tools, and the self-confidence you need to succeed."

Take the time to make the determination if business school is right for you.

Really think about it.

And if, at the end of that analysis, you conclude that business school is the next logical step for you, there is only one thing left to do:

Go for it!

ABOUT THE AUTHORS

ROBERT H. MILLER, thirty-one, graduated in May
1998 from the University of Pennsylvania Law
School, where he was a senior editor of the *University of Pennsylvania Law Review*, and H. Clayton
Louderback Legal Writing Instructor, and the Chairman of the
Executive Committee on Student Ethics and Academic Standing; and from Yale University in 1993. He is an attorney with
the law firm of Sheehan, Phinney, Bass & Green in Manchester,
New Hampshire, where he specializes in business and intellectual property litigation. He is the author of the critically acclaimed law school preparatory book, *Law School Confidential.*
Mr. Miller lives in the village of Hopkinton, New Hampshire,
with his wife, Carolyn, and son, Nicholas.

KATHERINE F. KOEGLER, twenty-eight, graduated
from Northwestern University's Kellogg Business
School in 2001, with concentrations in entrepreneurship, marketing, and finance. Prior to business school Ms. Koegler helped start and grow an e-commerce

business focused on improving patients' understanding of their illness and medical procedures and communication with their physician.

Ms. Koegler graduated from Yale University in 1996. She currently resides in Denver, Colorado.

15370925R00159

Made in the USA
Lexington, KY
23 May 2012